# Christian
# Ethics
# for **Black**
# Theology

# Christian Ethics for **Black** Theology

by

## MAJOR J. JONES

ABINGDON PRESS  Nashville • New York

CHRISTIAN ETHICS FOR BLACK THEOLOGY

*Library of Congress Cataloging in Publication Data*
JONES, MAJOR J        1919-
Christian ethics for Black theology.
Includes bibliographical references.
1. Christian ethics. 2. Negroes—Religion.
I. Title.
BJ1251.J63        241        74-8680
        *ISBN 0-687-07208-5*

MANUFACTURED BY THE PARTHENON PRESS AT
NASHVILLE, TENNESSEE, UNITED STATES OF AMERICA

# Preface

This book has grown out of my constant contact with and assessment of the writings and exchange of views of the current black theologians who are now contributing to the total theologizing process from a black theological frame of reference. A small facet of the ethical views expressed herein is a further elaboration on thoughts earlier projected in my first book, *Black Awareness: A Theology of Hope*. It is also an elaboration of lectures given at Emory University's Candler School of Theology in the summer of 1971, at Pittsburgh Theological Seminary, and the Southeastern Regional Meeting of the American Society of Christian Ethics in New Orleans on "The Ethical Problems in the Development of a Theology of revolution."

To be more specific, my reason for attempting such a book has grown out of my deep sense of the ethical and the seeming lack of a sense of the need for adequate ethical formulations or foundations on the part of so many persons who speak and write black theology from a somewhat negative point of view. One will note also a deep commitment to a conviction that the ethical question should be divided for the ex-master and the ex-slave, with the view that each has a respective responsibility to act from a different vantage point and in a different way.

These ethical formulations do not embrace the idea of reconciliation because the book takes the general position that the New Testament concept of reconciliation is not the relationship that is now being sought by black and white people in America; this is for the simple reason that the two races have never had an ideal prior relationship as is implied in the New Testament concept of reconciliation. Rather the book seeks to suggest ethical formulations necessary to build a totally new creative relationship that has never heretofore existed between black and white people in America.

Such a book would not have been possible without the friendship of the many people who teach in the Interdenominational Theological Center. They have provided a constant supply of inspiration and encouragement which has resulted in the content contained in this book. Without their prodding, no work of this sort could ever have been accomplished.

A special word of thanks goes to Dr. Grant S. Shockley of the Candler School of Theology faculty for the help he gave when progress was slow and when there was need for an exchange of views; more than mere recognition should go to my wife Mattie, who by inspiration, insight, and example gave content and meaning to many of the ideas and the more mature concepts that are set forth within these pages.

My thanks also go to a trusted friend, Mrs. Jessie H. Tucker, for her final manuscript suggestions; and to Mrs. Marian J. McDonald, my secretary, for her labor in typing the manuscript; and to the many publishers and authors who allowed me to quote from their books and periodicals.

MAJOR J. JONES

# Contents

PART TWO

# PART ONE_____

# I.
# The Case for a Division of the Ethical Question

## The Ethical Imperative

Now that so much has been written about black theology and it has been firmly established and generally accepted as a legitimate and necessary facet of the total theologizing process, it may well be time for black theologians to be addressing themselves to other areas of religious thought so long neglected by those who traditionally have been viewing theology from a too narrow frame of reference.

It is the intent of this book to move the discussion of black theology out further into the area of Christian ethics. It seeks to do so for the simple reason that whenever the oppressed black Christian, or indeed, the current black person (who may not even consider himself oppressed, as inconceivable as that may be) attempts to answer the moral or ethical question of "What ought I to do,"[1] he is likely to come up with a different answer derived from the same set of ethical criteria than would his counterpart who is white. If the answer to the same moral questions, derived from the same set of ethical criteria, principles, models, or values, are to be altered by what one has become or what he is as a person, then to be black in pro-white America is, perhaps, to be ethical in quite a different sense. It is to act ethically in a different way. Indeed, do not black people have to ask a different ethical question than do their white brothers about the nature and character of the moral self? Is the ethical mandate for the black and white Christian the same? If it is true that the basic assumptions and contentions of black theology are different from the broader scope of theology that is currently written from a totally white perspective, then it must also follow that Christian ethics or moral philosophy written from a white perspective would, in some sense, be different from Christian ethics or moral philosophy written from a black frame of reference.

The morally serious Christian may ask himself "What ought I to do?" in the midst of his concrete responsibilities and opportunities. The answer to this question depends on who is asking the question; and the answer may be made in light of what the person has become. If he is black, the answer might be one thing; if he is white, it might be quite another. Heretofore, Christian ethicists have not made such a distinction. This book contends that the ethical question "What ought I to do?" must be answered against the background of a personhood that is derived partly from the social context. Such a view is clearly stated by Walter Moberly when he contends that "any individual is what he is, not as a matter of merit or demerit. Ultimately, every person, and not only the social failure and the outcast, is the product of the psycho-

[1] James M. Gustafson, *Christ and the Moral Life* (New York: Harper & Row, 1968), p. 12.

physical construction with which he was born and of the society into which he was born."[2] If we take Moberly's above statements concerning personhood to be representative of the fact of being, then the black man can say with everybody else that he is only partly responsible for what he is; and, indeed, his responsibilities may be less. That is, if we take Moberly seriously when he further contends that "the individual's education, his recreations, his way of earning a livelihood, are determined by social institutions which seem to have acquired a momentum and an energy of their own."[3] However, when we place race into the process of becoming, and see how it has been used traditionally against black people, we can see that if the responsibility lies somewhere, it belongs to the whole of the American society of which the black man is only a subordinate part. If American society is partly responsible for the making of the advantaged white person, then the degree to which a black person is disadvantaged is the degree to which society is responsible for what he has become; and it is to that degree that the moral imperative is different for him. It is true that society is made up of persons, but "What ought I to do?" becomes both personal and social within every given context. This ethical responsibility varies according to the freedom and the power possessed by each of the individual participants in society as a whole.[4]

When one talks of the liberation of black people or of the changes needed to bring about social justice, the meaning is different for each individual. For the socially advantaged white person, it means yielding old privileges, accepting new risks, and giving up traditional positions of economic advantage. For the

---

[2] Walter Moberly, *Responsibility* (Greenwich, Conn.: The Seabury Press, 1956), p. 15.

[3] As quoted in L. Harold DeWolf's "Public and Private Dimensions of Ethical Responsibility," *Toward a Discipline of Social Ethics: Essays in Honor of Walter George Muelder* (Boston: Boston University Press, 1972), p. 284.

[4] *Ibid.*, p. 285.

socially disadvantaged black man, it means accepting a new social status, assuming new positions of power and responsibility, and acquiring a new sense of justice for those whom he had displaced as oppressors. As a black person who was once suppressed, he would now have to deal with his newly acquired powers. He would now have to determine whether he would use his newly acquired powers to empower others or to suppress them. "What ought I to do?" would be quite different now than it was before when he was the oppressed. To know what he ought to do now should be reassessed ethically in the light of whom he has now become.

So, to repeat, it is the contention of this book that the ethical question of "What ought I to do?" needs to be divided and that an answer to such an ethical question needs to be attempted from both the black and white ethical frames of reference. It may well be that the ethical problems in relation to black and white relations are centered in the fact that those who have traditionally written Christian ethics have heretofore attempted to be too general in their ethical formulations. Though the basic assumptions may be that the issues which concern theologians who write about ethics and morality are no different from other ethics, it is still the core belief of this book that there is a polarity of moral judgments clustered about the black and white issues within the context of pro-white America. This makes it mandatory that some attempt be made to formulate a system of ethics more applicable to the existential condition of each racial group as they struggle from their respective vantage points to find a collective good life as human beings. This is an attempt to speak ethically from the black side of the question. These ethical formulations are written for the American race problem because, while there may be a world problem, the American racial problem is unique.

If it is only the love ethics of *agapé* to which ultimate Christian ethics call both black and white Christians, then Paul Ramsey is right when he says:

An unbinding love would seem the least likely conclusion one would reach if he seriously regarded the freedom of God's love in binding Himself to the world as the model for all covenants between men. Could anyone who perceives that God in total love and total freedom bound Himself to the world possibly view the implications of this love as unbinding on men? Love seems to have only a dissolving or relativising power when the *freedom of agapé* is taken to mean love's *inability* to bind itself one way and not another or in no way except in acts that are the immediate response of one person's depth to another's depth.[5]

However, taken in its ultimate connoted meaning, as Ramsey's above statement would indicate, when such an absolute rule of love is applied to the ex-master–ex-slave relationship, the ex-master and the ex-slave are bound by the same moral imperative; but the implementations of the same ethical mandate may be different. If it is true, as Plato has indicated, "that the tyrant is himself a slave, [then] the enslavement of another is also the enslavement of oneself."[6] Then, it follows that for each of them to meet the higher mandate of love, they each must acquire different kinds of mind-sets and choose different paths.

The act of liberation, be it external or internal, must restore to each one his spiritual nature or his higher humanity; each must become aware of himself as a free person and a spiritual being. In this sense, freedom is not only derived from the masters, but it is also derived from the slaves,[7] and for these two the ethical mandates are different. Indeed, just as the two paths to a common freedom are different, so is the ethical mandate for the slave different from the ethical mandate for the master. Such is true because there is still a carry-over of the slave-master mind-set within the mentality of the black man and the white man. Indeed,

[5] Paul Ramsey, Deeds and Rules in Christian Ethics (New York: Charles Scribner's Sons, 1967), pp. 127-28.

[6] Quoted in Nikolai Berdyaev, *Slavery and Freedom* (New York: Charles Scribner's Sons, 1944), p. 61.

[7] *Ibid.*

19

as Dr. Vincent Harding puts it, "At the heart of the matter . . . is the issue of how we can prepare Black people to live with integrity on the scene of our former enslavement and our present estrangement."[8]

The basic ethical problem is posed on the tripartite conceptions of the ex-slave, oppressed, black man and the ex-master, oppressor white man, because while the black-white relationship has moved far beyond the point of legal slavery and to some much milder forms of legal oppression, there still exists much of the slave-master, oppressed-oppressor, mentality in the mind-set of both black and white people. The slave-master mentality clouds all race relations in America to a point where it is almost impossible for the two races to achieve a climate wherein they both can treat each other as equals.

Albert Camus divides the master-slave question this way:

> The slave revolts against the master. He denies him as a master, but not as a man. For his protest is directed against the master's refusal to treat him as a man. As master and slave, neither is a true man and neither can relate to the other in a humane way. If the denial of the master were total, the slave's revolt would bring nothing new into the world but would only exchange the roles of inhumanity.[9]

The ideal ethical task of the slave, the oppressed, or the black man should not be to turn the slave into a master, an oppressed person into an oppressor, or a black man into a mere hater of white people; rather, it should be to subvert and abolish the whole master-slave, oppressed-oppressor, or black-white relationship so that in the future black men and white men will be able to treat each other as men—while still remaining black and white. Under such a moral obligation, each has his respective response. To

[8] Vincent Harding, "The Religion of Black Power," *The Religious Situation* (Boston: Beacon Press, 1968), p. 20.

[9] As quoted in Jurgen Moltmann's, *Religion, Revolution and the Future* (New York: Charles Scribner's Sons, 1969) pp. 142-43.

overcome such a past is an ethical task that cannot be long overlooked. Black people have changed to such a degree that the ultimate demand is at hand. Now is the time in America for a new black-white relationship that has never before existed.

Indeed, if the ethical question "What ought I to do?" did not exist in the mind of either the master or the slave, the oppressed or the oppressor, the white man or the black man, the reason for such ethical formulations would not be needed.

## Christian Ethics and a Sense of Moral Obligation

It has been argued by some Christian moralists that the sense of obligation has no place in the Christian moral ideal.[10] The idea of the "should," it is said, is a legalistic conception that is not related to the Christian ethical mandate. Indeed, one would suppose if this were true that there would be no need for this more specialized divided approach to Christian ethics. For, as they contend, the idea of "should" points to a law which we are obligated to obey, and through which alone we can attain a sense of inner satisfaction. It is true that between what "should be" and the "what is" there is a necessary gulf. It is also true that the "should" refers to something which does not exist; and if it did exist, there would be no sense of the "should" in connection with it. It must also be conceded that the realization of "should" cancels the should.

However, such a cancellation, as far as our total moral life is concerned, cannot be achieved unless we are totally committed and unless we concede that the ideal is not a futuristic concept. In this sense, it always imposes upon us a perpetual sense of obligation, and we are kept in permanent bondage to the "should."

In relation to the central concerns of this book, there are two things that should be kept in mind. First of all, whether we

[10] Cf. Emil Brunner, *The Divine Imperative* (New York: Macmillan, 1937), pp. 34, 93.

conceive of the "should" from the objective moral-law level or from the subjective act-oriented level, the ethical "should" is related to a deep human yearning; indeed, it is related to a dream that cannot be deferred. It has to do with "what is" as well as with what should be, and hence it transcends what is by its very mandate. It is, then, clear that the moral law with its "should be" does not exclude, but in a larger measure *includes* that which is.

Secondly, it must be kept in mind that this "should" deals with a hunger deeper than yearning or normal conduct; it deals with acts or actions in relation to other human beings and their freedom to be. Thus, being itself is at stake; and what one does, in relation to the "should" may well determine what we will become as well as what another may be allowed to become. Probably no person has expressed this deep yearning and hunger better than C. Eric Lincoln:

> This is the era of the "hungry man to some, The Abominable Hungry Man." The hungry man is the symbol of very many millions of people who are hungry for food, hungry for understanding, hungry for freedom and self-determination. But most of all—hungry for the dignity without which a man is a . . . misfit, a monstrous joke in his own eyes. A broken vessel in the eyes of God.
> The sign of the hungry man is his determination, his dedication, his quiet insistence, and his courage. It is the sign of the search for dignity.[11]

From the white perspective, Emil Brunner asserts it in another, more general way. "The true being of man, therefore, can mean nothing else than standing in the love of God, being drawn into His love of man. Or, to put it differently, it means living a life which, from its source in God, is directed toward man, toward the interest of others."[12]

[11] C. Eric Lincoln, *Sounds of the Struggle* (New York: Friendship Press, 1967), p. 86.

[12] Brunner, *The Divine Imperative,* pp. 34, 93.

Surely it is also related to Paul Ramsey's statement concerning a binding love which related man to man in a binding love relation to God. For Brunner and Ramsey, man is related to man by being conjointly bound together in God's love. However, to return to the basic thesis of the book, holding that the ethical question should be divided, one gets the feeling that neither Brunner nor Ramsey are talking about the same ethical mandate as would be seen in Lincoln's statement speaking of man's hunger for self-fulfillment. And if they were, would there not be a difference in the way love's binding process would have to be achieved? Until white and black people both transcended the master-slave level of relationships, they would each approach the higher level from his own respective status. [13]

The black Christian who answers the ethical "should" in the affirmative in relation to the slave-master problem with the ethical incentive to subvert and abolish such an unequal relationship will have to proceed against the background of a past history with his former slaveholder. He must also realize that a part of the slave mentality is carried over into the oppressed-oppressor relationship, and it is further interspersed into the current black-white relationship. This is one of the reasons why it is so hard to eradicate racism from the American scene. That is what the black experience is all about, and it is why this book is so narrow in its scope.

However, a more cogent problem is that of the necessary ethical incentive on the part of either black or white people to perfect such a relationship beyond the racism of yesteryear. From both sides there must come an answer to the question of what to do to perfect a better tomorrow. The ultimate answer must be totally void of the slave-master, oppressed-oppressor, or black-white polarity. The ethical question, then, divides at the point of whether or not the ex-slave, oppressed black people want to

[13] Albert C. Knudson, *The Principles of Christian Ethics* (Nashville: Abingdon Press, 1953), pp. 74 ff.

perfect a mutual relationship with ex-master, oppressing white people.

If the answer is in the affirmative, then this book is offered as an exploration of some of the ethical issues confronting the black side, with some broader implications for the white side. For in a real sense, on the relational slope which black men and white men are scaling, it should always be the moral imperative, whether derived from a subjective or an objective ethical incentive, that guides the "I-Thou" relationship upward toward a more humane climate of mutual acceptance and respect. If, after having adhered to the mandate of such an imperative, after each has been completely liberated through the many stages of renewal, each should acquire no other goal but to relate to each other at the point of such a relational summit wherein each will have no other motive but mutual endeavor. Only at the point of the summit may they each know what it means to enjoy and share a common path. Only then may they regret that their prior ways to the summit needed to be different and that the time span was so long. However, as with Camus, they may each conclude that "the struggle itself toward the heights was enough to fill a man's heart."

# II.
# Human Nature and the Moral Imperative in Black and White

## An Educational View of Human Nature

The approach to black Christian ethics is intimately related to ethical conceptions of human nature. How one views human nature is surely related to how one conceives of his ethical obligation—whether the obligation is derived from an objective or a subjective moral incentive. The fact that one is black or white further relates the moral incentive to his ethical view of self. Traditionally, there have been four possible conceptions of human nature, each having something to do with how one approaches the formulations or the study of Christian ethics.

First of all, there is a view which holds that human nature, in its essence, is good and that the focus of evil is outside man. This does not mean that people are universally good or that the good exceeds the evil in man. To contend such would be to overlook or dismiss the obvious perversions and shortcomings to which people are actually subject. However, in affirming the essential goodness of man, this view is simply claiming that the evil which is made manifest in man is not inherent in his true nature; it is contending that evil is a denial and a contradiction of that nature. It is to assert that a human being is less human when he is evil than when he is good. The evil is subhuman or antihuman. The true selfhood of a person is good, and whatever is evil is not one's true self. According to this position, if a person is unhappy, it is because he has not found himself. If he is ignorant, it is because he has not been given the chance or the means to acquire an education, and it is because he has not been given the opportunity to fulfill his true nature. If one is dishonest or uncooperative, he is not true to himself or to others. Such a view is an affirmation of the fact that even within the most vicious and depraved person there remains a spark of essential goodness that can always be appealed to and, with care, can be fanned into a full flame of goodness.

Indeed, this school of ethics would hold that there is within all persons an unfolding tendency toward the good, and much of what is labeled evil is simply a misdirection of that natural tendency toward the good. Hate, for example, is held to be the result of frustrated love. All persons want desperately to establish relationships of affectionate mutuality with other persons, but circumstances prevent it, and the disappointment felt at this failure finds expression in the angered response called hate. There would, according to this view, be no hate were there not a prior and continuing concern to be in relationship with others. The opposite of love is not hate, but, rather, unconcern, estrangement, and alienation.

Again, the many forms of dishonesty can be regarded as misguided attempts to attain the good. The conduct of a person is always governed by the apparent good. No one, according to this view, knowingly chooses evil. Man is fundamentally good at heart, and it is only necessary that he be well informed. If the good is clearly evident to a person, he will do it.

If nature, as this view would assess it, is essentially good, the function of moral education would be to recognize and encourage that goodness. It would be the duty of those who educate to provide the right interpretation, the right understanding and conceptualization of those actions. Then innate strivings which lead to fulfillment and then ultimate self-realization can succeed. The acquisition of knowledge is also an important objective of moral education, since only the informed person will be able to avoid mistaken ways of carrying out his good intentions. Whether one is black or white may make the difference in how he or she is educated in America.

Secondly, there is the view which holds that the many and obvious evils of life are not merely accidents or mistakes, but are integrally rooted in the very nature and stuff of man. This is not to deny that there is not some goodness in human beings. The manifest virtues in such qualities as love, sacrifice, creativity, and devotion to truth are too obvious to permit a wholly adverse judgment. But those who would hold this point of view would contend that such goodness is not of man's own nature; it is rather grafted upon or into him by some external source—either by moral education, social experience, or some other superhuman agency. To become human is essentially to be evil. To become good is to become social or superhuman. The real self must be overcome since it is selfish, cruel, and domineering. It must be replaced by a new self and informed by the ethical content which is clearly understood and adhered to. This school of thought would further contend that, unfortunately, even much of what is viewed as good in persons is but disguised evil.

27

To view man or human nature as evil, one must conclude that human virtue is purely external or hypocritical. It may be external in the sense that morality is an imposed code whose purpose is to check and channel the evil impulses of men. It is hypocritical to the extent that persons represent goodness as their own, using virtue as a mask for their own evil designs. Thus, the mere profession of high ideals is merely to put up a good front, representing oneself as something other than the true self.

Moral knowledge, then, is to help man to suppress his natural evil tendencies and to replace them with more desirable ones. To be educated, then, is to appear to be what one really is not. In the education of evil men, then, knowledge cannot be freely given and cannot be entrusted to all, but only to those who have proved themselves submissive to the restraints which moral education puts upon their evil tendencies. Then who would ultimately become the fully educated, if racism is to be one standard of education?

A third view of human nature combines the first two and holds that man is essentially both good and evil. To say that man is essentially both good and evil is not the same as saying that he is essentially good, but has fallen into some evil ways; nor is it to contend that he is essentially evil, but has developed some good qualities. It is not simply to affirm that in some respects or at one time a person is good and in other respects, or at other times, evil. It is not to assert that man is a mere mixture of good and evil characteristics. It is, rather, to contend that at the core of his being, man is at once and in the same respects both good and evil. Man is, thus, ambiguous. He manifests no generosity void of some elements of pride. Devotion to truth is never totally and completely free of bias and special pleading. Moral structiveness is not inseparable from imperiousness. Love and hate are not separate, but are inextricably intermixed. Man's very goodness may well occasion evil. His essential goodness may well become a captive of his essential evil. For this school of thought, there is within human nature itself a deep cleft and an inescapable contradiction.

Moral education for this school of thought cannot eliminate the essential ambiguity within human nature: the good and the evil tendencies will grow and develop together. Appeals must be made to the deep resources or creativity, while taking care that the evil tendencies are not encouraged to develop. In every evil tendency, the moral educator must endeavor to see and utilize the implicit good, and in every good he must be alert to the possible implicit evil.

Finally, the fourth view of human nature is that it is neutral: that it is neither good nor evil, but is capable of becoming either or both. Man is what he has become. There are some persons who are vicious and depraved, and there are others who have become saintly. According to the neutral view, there is nothing innately good or innately evil about man. He has the capacity to become either good or evil; it is largely a matter of choice.

It is interesting to note that those who contend that man is essentially good or evil, or both, differ from the neutral position on one or more points. This view contends first that while there are great differences in individuals and in cultures, there is an underlying human nature which is common to all but which operates differently in various situations and contexts. Secondly, they assert that there is a universally applicable moral standard. Some locate the standard in natural law while others locate it in deity, but all accept it as a standard which can be used to judge whether human beings are good or evil.

For the fourth view, if human nature is neutral, moral education then becomes of basic importance in the making of persons, for it is education and not some innate quality that determines what a person is to become. Given some standard of value, the task of moral education is to produce persons who are good by that standard. Good persons are products of good education, and thus evil people result from poor education. Since there are no evil tendencies to suppress, the methods of education may be positive and direct. Since there is no innate goodness to express, the educator cannot merely encourage inherent creative powers, but must explicitly demonstrate and inspire desired outcomes. Knowledge is neither good nor bad in itself. It rather derives its worth from its use for valued ends. Black people have been right in contending that much of American education has been used as a means of control as the above would suggest. They are right in contending that education tends to determine what a person may become. However, it must be concluded that education is necessary if one is to be the kind of person suggested by this book.

## A Theological View of Human Nature

The four views of human nature are descriptive in their attempt to give a nonreligious, moral, educational approach to human nature. However, if one is to understand the meaning of human nature as to why man acts as he does, then he must turn to the theological explanation. Yet one cannot overlook the fact that the descriptive views of human nature have deep implications for black Christian ethics.

It is the position of this book that man, whether black or white, is neither a saint nor a sinner. Man has an innate capacity for both good and evil. Man is not neutral; rather he is born with equal tendencies toward both the good and the bad. He is fully capable, by decision, of becoming what he wills to become. Man is unique as an act of God's creation. He was created a finite being, a child of nature, and as such is involved in the necessities of the natural order like all other created things. But more than other facets of God's creation, man was also created a spiritual being existing in a personal relationship with God—a free rational being with the capacity to have knowledge of and a fellowship with God. In this respect, man is different from other living things, and he is preeminent among them. But these same capacities and endowments, which are the mark of man's grandeur, are also the marks of his misery. It is man alone who can become a sinner; it is only man who can fall from the state of innocence in which he is created. It is man alone who can become a saint.

Christianity is right in affirming that there is something wrong with man which affects him to the very core of his being. Not only are many of his actions distorted and corrupted, but seemingly his fundamental relationship to God has, at times, become perverted. Consequently, according to this view, man is out of harmony with himself, with others, and with God. Looking at what man ought to be under God, looking at man realistically as he so often has become through sin, Reinhold Niebuhr was right in asserting that "Christianity measures the status of man more highly and his virtue more severely than any other alternative view."[1]

Such a theological view of man is but an affirmation of man's capacity and striving for wholeness and for harmony with nature, with his fellows, and with God. Indeed, these biblical and theological concepts imply further that the struggle for such wholeness and harmony is an integral part of the divine creative process. They also imply that man can be harmoniously related to himself, to nature, to others—only if he is harmoniously related to God. As David E. Rogers puts it:

> The resources he draws upon, in seeking to become at one with himself, are not merely "his"; they are rooted in the whole of creation, which is grounded in God. Therefore, man can become at one with himself only by finding his place in a harmony much wider than himself; but this harmony is not "preestablished"; he has a share in winning, in actualizing it. He cannot fulfill his own nature unless his capacities gain free expression; but neither can he fulfill his own nature unless his freedom is brought into the right relationship with God.[2]

[1] Reinhold Niebuhr, *The Nature and Destiny of Man: Human Nature* (New York: Charles Scribner's Sons, 1943), I, 161.

[2] David E. Roberts, *Psychotherapy and a Christian View of Man* (New York: Charles Scribner's Sons, 1950), p. 93.

The Christian faith is right in its rejection of vitalism as a valid view of mankind. It must be recognized that there is a need for discipline and restraint in man's exercise of his biological drives—which are not to be viewed as evil per se. The Christian faith may not affirm egocentricity, but it does not condemn pride in the sense of one trusting in his own abilities and works. It does not regard man's longing or yearning to improve his state of existence as sin. Sin does not belong to man's essential nature. If it did, we could not affirm that Christ was truly man. But, we cannot overlook the fact that all other actual human beings are sinful. Thus, Paul Tillich speaks of sin as the universal estrangement of our existence from our essense. The ultimate purpose of our striving as human beings is to become (and enable or extend to our neighbors the freedom to become) human.

We are free, but we are estranged in our freedom. We regard our freedom as God's gift from his own infinitely greater freedom, a sharing of his own nature, a part of the divine image. This freedom, or life, is to be understood further as a breathing of God's own creativity into ourselves and others. It is where we meet God in existence; it is life's growing edge held close to its author's own will in committed obedience. This is life at the rare moments of its best when it is fully aware of its higher aim and purpose. Too often life withers in the self-centered estrangement from God. It is this state of estrangement that needs a theological explanation. It is to such an explanation that we now direct our attention.

## The Ethical Significance of the Fall

There are at least four interpretations of the Fall that should be cited in this context that are important for the central concern of this book and for our current understanding of human nature.

First, there are those who take the story of the Fall in Genesis 3 to be a historical event, a literal truth, of Adam's actual act of sin; and, as a result of his sin, they contend that all men are sinners.

Before the Fall, man had the ability to sin or not to sin. However, since the Fall neither Adam nor any of his subsequent descendants possessed the same prior freedom or the ability not to sin. Indeed, according to this point of view, as a result of the Fall, both Adam and all his posterity have had only the ability to sin.

Secondly, modern Augustinians such as Reinhold Niebuhr, Emil Brunner, and most neo-orthodox theologians reject a literalistic historical account of the fall of Adam from a state of holiness into a state of sin and guilt through the act of eating the forbidden fruit of a certain tree. They reject the notions of a historical hereditary corruption of human nature and the biological transmission of guilt. They reject such notions because these views undermine man's freedom and moral responsibility. Insofar as they speak of a corruption that is inherited, they speak more of it as being inherited historically and socially in terms of personal relationships that have been distorted, rather than in terms of some sort of concept which holds that the very stuff of the flesh, the biological substance of being itself, became tainted by the Fall. Though they may reject the literal interpretation of the Fall, they do not accept fully the rejection of the idea of sin. Indeed, Niebuhr teaches not only a doctrine of sin, but a doctrine of original sin, which he centers in the will rather than in the flesh. Sin, Niebuhr claims, is universal in mankind. For him, there is a universal tendency toward sin, and this makes sin inevitable. Although sin is inevitable, it is not necessary; thus, man is free to choose the good or the evil. Man sins in freedom, and he is fully responsible for his actions. Man is a creature, a sinful creature; but he is also a free spirit able to transcend nature and to make history.[3]

Thirdly, there is a view of the Fall, often called the "Myth of Adam" as the writers of the book of Genesis presented it. This view would not totally reject the theological interpretation of the Fall as representative of what is wrong with man, if anything is

[3] Niebuhr, *The Nature and Destiny of Man: Human Nature*, I, 261 ff.

wrong with him. It is, rather, a descriptive, and the fall of Adam and Eve is viewed as mere myth, not to be taken seriously. While they do not totally reject sin, they opt for more freedom.

Finally, if we look at the Genesis story with clear minds, we will find a deep truth that is quite different from the meaning of a myth. It is not by accident that this classic story portraying the birth of human consciousness and maturity is a myth explaining mankind's tendency to revolt against God, asserting his independence and freedom. Before the Fall, under the "benevolent dictatorship" of God, Adam and Eve existed in a state of naïve, prehuman happiness, a contentment without anxiety, shame, or conflict; they existed like an infant in the early months of life, completely without moral or mature individual consciousness. Subsequently, Adam and Eve then go through steps parallel to a child's developmental stages. They question authority (symbolized in the questions projected to the serpent); they experience moral consciousness (partaking of the fruit of the tree of the knowledge of good and evil). The price they pay for their revolt against the authority of God is shame, guilt, anxiety, conflict, and final ejection from the blissful, infant state of the Garden of Eden. As Milton pictures for us in *Paradise Lost:*

> The world was all before them, where to choose
> Their place of rest, the Providence their guide.
> They, hand in hand, with wandering steps and slow,
> Through Eden took their solitary way.

What was their gain as they said goodbye to Eden? They gained differentiation of themselves as persons—the beginning of identity. They also gained the possibility of passion and human creativity. In place of the naïve, nonresponsible dependencies of infancy, there is now the possibility of loving by choice. There is now the chance of relating to one's fellowmen because one wants to, and hence with responsibility. The myth of Adam is, as Hegel put it, a "fall upward." It is, indeed, the emergence of mature consciousness.

While one might agree with Hegel that Adam and Eve fell upward, one must take seriously the fact that the Fall is one of the best explanations that has ever been given in the whole of literature as an attempt to make sense out of much that is contrary to what ought to be man's true nature. It may be that the insights of Ruth Nanda Anshen are more suggestive when she contends that what happened in the Devil's fall was that "it was only after his fall from grace, after God's damnation for a not-yet Satanic disobedience, that Lucifer embraced evil and diabolically devoted himself to the eternal hatred of God."[4]

Indeed, it could have been that in man's fall upward, he also acquired the ability to fall either way, upward or downward. Whenever mankind embraces evil, he falls downward, and whenever he embraces good, he falls upward. He is always free to do either; the choice is his. The nature of the good or the evil determines the nature, the direction, and the extent of the fall.

## American Slavery and the Fall

If one looks at the history of American slavery, he must conclude that so great was the evil of institutional slavery until neither white nor black Americans have fully recovered. The black man has not fully recovered from what he allowed slavery to do to him, and the white man has not fully recovered from what he permitted himself to do to a people. Suggested means of recovery for the black man is the central theme of this book.

## Ethical Implications of Human Nature and Power

Probably no theologian in the twentieth century has had a clearer ethical understanding of power than the late Reinhold Niebuhr. His views of the nature of man's role in the use of power in the political arena have dominated Christian social ethics for

[4] Ruth Nanda Anshen, *The Reality of the Devil: Evil in Man* (New York: Harper & Row, 1972), p. 11.

almost half a century. Man, in Niebuhr's view, is a finite creature whose nature bridges animal vitalities and self-transcendence, with a faith enabling him to live creatively in a tension between the two. In man's social and political life, Niebuhr sees arrogance manifesting itself in self-love and the will-to-power, with man's natural egotistic inclinations compounded in group life. In Niebuhr's opinion the corruption of power grows out of the struggle in man's inner nature between freedom and finitude. The inevitable consequences of man's arrogance with egotism is exacerbated in the collective life. If one applies Niebuhr's understanding of pride and the use of power to the black-white relation as was exampled in the black experience in America, he must conclude that slavery was a fall.

After reading the account of the Fall, after having assessed human nature in the light of the plight of black people, one can only conclude that this is why it is so difficult to eradicate the white man's tendency toward power and the sinful use to which he has put that power. There are many reasons why slavery represents a modern day fall for the white man. In the first place, in the whole history of the human race, no other people have directed their pride and power at another people in quite the same way as the white man did against the black man in America. The white man's pride has dominated the whole black-white relationship since the beginning of the days of slavery. One needs only to look at American history to see that the white-dominated society is one in which the assertion of the white self involves a total denial of the black self. It has been traditionally so arrogant as to contend, at times, that the black man was less than human simply because he was black and of another culture. Such a view has also made the white elite almost unteachable in relation to the humanity of black people—otherwise why would there be racism? The essence of pride is the distrust of the audience, especially if the audience is black. Pride of color and pride of his historical advantages over the current black man have traditionally kept the white man in power; and this power is but a manifestation of his pride. It has also been a manifestation of his pride in who he is and what he thinks himself to be.

The quest for black liberation will end with the self-empowerment of the now powerless black people so that they may have the power to participate in all decisions affecting their welfare and fulfillment. The black man must achieve a counter power to offset the current power of the collective white society. He must of necessity empower himself; this power will never be given to him.

As has been pointed out above, the greatest fall downward in modern times was the downward fall of the white man during the dark days of slavery. Human nature was at its worst, and those who were victims were both the black and white people who now struggle with the lingering problems. That the institution of slavery was made legitimate by religion and justified as ethically and morally right has had a great and lasting effect on American thinking. The traditional attitudes toward the slave still suffer greatly because of the traditional attitudes of the master, who has not yet given up his belief that he is better than the black man therefore should remain in an advantaged position with a majority power. Pride and a mixture of religious beliefs sustain such convictions. If the above view had not become theological and moral, it may well not have been considered a fall. However, the fact that it did made it, indeed, a fall.

George F. Thomas makes pride the "root of some, if not all of the other sins." Thomas further concludes, concerning man's pride, that while he "refuses to acknowledge his inferiority to God, he also will not admit his equality with men. Slavery has made it hard for both black and white people to accept each other as equals. From the perspective of religion and morality alike, pride is the greatest sin."[5]

[5] George F. Thomas, *Christian Ethics and Moral Philosophy* (New York: Charles Scribner's Sons, 1955), pp. 188-89.

This superior pride is the thing most difficult for people of like physical characteristics to overcome; but when there is a physical difference, it is almost impossible. It is this superficial difference between blackness and whiteness that forms what seems to be the greatest barrier against the black man.

# III.
# Christian Ethics in Historical Perspective

## Christian Ethics and Black Theology

Christian ethics is currently under broad attacks, perhaps as it has never been before. First, there are those who would like to abandon Christian ethics as a standard for moral conduct. Secondly, there are those who would like to reinterpret Christian ethics in the light of what they would call more modern standards of conduct. Those who would reinterpret Christian ethics would do so in an attempt to reduce standards for conduct to what is more acceptable and easy. Thirdly, there are still others who would have little regard for the basic objective formulations of traditional Christian ethics; they would rather relate what one ought to do to the existential context and to one's own status of

39

being within that context. They contend that if there are values or principles which determine what one ought to do, these values or principles are but the creation of man; they have no reality apart from the willing subject. The structure of values chosen from this third point of view arises within the individual alone, or within the collective social context, and they correspond to nothing whatever in a supposedly objective order.

However, those who dismiss Christian ethics so lightly need to be called back to the basic Christian heritage, if for no other reason than to be reminded that those who in the past have lost their way ethically have also lost their way socially, politically, and otherwise. As one reads much of the current formulations of both black and white theology, he is impressed that too little attention is given to the ethical traditions of the Christian faith, and that much more emphasis is placed on the current existential historical context. Indeed, black theology tends, at times, to define its understanding as to what one should do in the light of a total this-world context. James H. Cone contends that:

> The revolutionary situation forces Black Theology to shun all abstract principles dealing with what is the "right" and "wrong" course of action. There is only one principle which guides the thinking and actions of Black Theology, an unqualified commitment to the Black community as that community seeks to define its existence in the light of God's liberating work in the world. This means that Black Theology refuses to be guided by ideas and concepts alien to Black people.[1]

Does Cone really mean what he seems to be saying? To the contrary, no Christian ethics, or Christian theology for that matter, can be fully Christian without giving due regard to the ethical tradition of the faith. It is important for this work on black Christian ethics, as it attempts to provide broader ethical formulations for black theology and the politics of liberation, to take a

---

[1] James H. Cone, *A Black Theology of Liberation* (Philadelphia: J. B. Lippincott, 1970), p. 33.

look at traditional Christian ethics to see if it is binding on the oppressed black person as he seeks to liberate himself from his oppressor. Because, under God, the actions employed by the oppressed black man may well mean the difference between his success or his failure.

## The Old Testament Roots of Black Christian Ethics

For the Old Testament, ethics is the conformity of human activity to the will of God. First of all, ethics for the Old Testament is not what convention tells one to do, but what God commands one to do.[2] Secondly, as William Barclay puts it:

> The ethics for the Old Testament are rooted in history. There is one thing that no Jew will ever forget—that his people were slaves in the land of Egypt and that God redeemed them. To this day that story is told and retold at every Passover time. "You must remember that you were a slave in the land of Egypt and that the Lord your God rescued you" (Deuteronomy 7:18; 8:2; 15:5; 16:12; 24:18, 22). That is the very keynote of Old Testament Religion.[2]

To give God some credit for what he has done is good for man—matters not who he is. To do so also means that one obligates himself to some standard set by God. Barclay also points out that this story is an account of the great works which God has done on behalf of a people. First, God has a right to speak to his people because he has done great things for them. The Jew would say God has a right to tell him how to behave, for God has shown that he can act with power—and act with power for him.

One can clearly see that within the Old Testament the idea of ethics is tied with and related to the idea of a covenant. Within this context, it must be noted that a covenant is more than a

[2] William Barclay, *Ethics in a Permissive Society* (New York: Harper & Row, 1971), p. 14.

[3] *Ibid,* pp. 14, 15.

bargain, an agreement, or a mere treaty between two people; for these latter would but place God on the same level with man. As Barclay puts it:

> The whole point of the covenant is that the whole initiative is with God. The idea is that God out of sheer grace—not because the nation of Israel was specially great or specially good—simply because he wanted to do it—came to Israel and said that they would be his people and he would be their God (Deuteronomy 7:6-8; 9:4,5).
>
> But the very act of grace brings its obligation. It laid on Israel the obligation for ever to try to be worthy of this choice of God.[4]

The one thing about which the Jews are collectively sure is the fact that they are the chosen people of God; that in some clear sense they specially and uniquely belong to God. They contend that he regards them in a special way. It must be recalled that to be chosen, therefore, is not to be free of a sense of obligation; it is, rather, to be that much more bound by that obligation to act like God's chosen people. To be chosen, then, brings one to a feeling of a heavy and terrifying sense of responsibility.

It is interesting that traditionally black people have considered themselves as God's chosen people, and at no other point in history has this theme been espoused as in the current expressions of the black man's liberation struggle. However, it comes to focus in two different ways. First, black people are told that we are to set an example in the role of the passive sufferer, yet not merely accepting our lot. Dr. King puts it this way:

> This is the challenge. If we will dare to meet it honestly, historians in future years will have to say that there lived a great people—a black people—who bore their burdens of oppression in the heat of many days and who, through tenacity and creative commitment, injected new meaning into the veins of American life.[5]

[4] *Ibid.*, p. 15.

[5] Martin Luther King, Jr., *Where Do We Go From Here: Chaos or Community?* (New York; Harper & Row, 1967), p. 134.

Secondly, black people are told that they must take their freedom by whatever means they deem necessary. Ronald Fair contends, in quite this sense, that:

> We are the ones who will right all the wrongs perpetrated against us and our ancestors, and we are the ones who will save the world and bring in a new day, a brilliantly alive society that swings and sings and rings out the world over for decency and honesty and sincerity and understanding and beauty and love.[6]

Indeed, this book takes the position that black people are God's chosen people. It is a fact that black people have, more than white America will admit, currently become the most important people within the context of American life. It may well be that from the inception of American slavery, black people became chosen people simply because of what that has meant to them as a slave. It is quite reasonable to contend also that the black people have been chosen by God because of what they have meant to their masters. One can even agree, while not fully accepting his self-concept of chosenness, that the black man has, by his mere presence in America, made a great difference in the life-style of the American white man. In spite of himself, the oppressor has been linked to the oppressed in America as in no other cultural or historical context. In this sense, for white America, the attempt to enslave the black man in such a way as to deny his total humanity, was indeed, a kind of spiritual fall. It is sad to say that such was a mutual dehumanizing process which hardened and degraded almost everyone who by choice or by force engaged in it. It has been a kind of millstone about the neck of all white people who would have made much greater cultural and spiritual progress had it not been for slavery and its aftermath. So, like black Afro-Americans, white Americans have never quite recovered from the evils of slavery.

[6] Ronald Fair, "Symposium on Black Power," *The Negro Digest* (Nov., 1966), p. 94.

To consider black people as a chosen people is to say one thing to their oppressors, but it is to speak to black people as the oppressed people in quite another sense. In a real sense, God cannot say to the black man, "You only have I known of all the families of the earth; therefore I will punish you for all of your iniquities" (Amos 3:2). God cannot say to black people that the greater their privilege, the greater their responsibility. For the better a chance God gives a people, the more blameworthy the people are if they fail him. However, there is a message from God for both black and white Americans. It is one of the most dreadful current ethical mandates of our time. "You have I chosen —therefore, you will I punish." As former master and as former slave, yet each not fully free, I now punish you both. The white man for what he has done to black people, the black man for what he has allowed the white man to do to him.

To be chosen is to be obedient. No chosen people can ever forget the obligations which Old Testament ethics suggest that God places upon any people who are among his chosen. Moses reminds the chosen of his day: "This day you have become the people of the Lord your God. You shall therefore, obey the voice of the Lord your God, keeping his commandments and his statutes" (Deut. 27:9-10). Not chosen and exempted from obedience, but rather chosen to be even more obliged to be an obedient people of God.

According to Old Testament ethics, this obedience was and still is of the very essence of life; the law which must be obeyed becomes, for the Jew and all others, the most important thing in life. As Moses said of the law in his farewell speech to the people: "It is no trifle for you, it is your life" (Deut. 32:47). It was through the law that they knew the will of God and that the necessary obedience must be rendered.

Such a conception of obedience had one obvious consequence; if accepted, the Jews had to be prepared to be different from all other nations. The word of God was quite clear at this point; they

44

were not to be like the Egyptians they were leaving, and they were not to be like the Canaanites into whose land they were going (Lev. 18:1-5, 20:23-24). God had separated them from other people.

Here we come to the central meaning of Jewish religion. The voice which they heard came to them again and again saying: You shall be holy because I am holy (Lev. 20:7, 26; 19:2; 11:44; 45). The basic Old Testament meaning of the word "holy" is different. The Jewish sabbath was holy because it was different from all other days of the week. It was different because one was to do different things on this day. The Bible is holy because it is different from all other books; the temple was holy because it was different from all other building. God is supremely holy because God is supremely different from all other gods. So, the very duty of the Jew is to be different; he is separated, he is chosen, he is God's, and, therefore, he is different from all other people. This ethical mandate is not a part of black theology. This should be one of the central themes of the black church.

One is not too sure that even Fanon, who is so widely read in the black community, at the end of his book *The Wretched of the Earth*[7] calls black people to quite the kind of exclusiveness to which the Jews were called in the Old Testament. Fanon, and others who now call black people to a kind of chosen separateness, call for a kind of separateness that is almost totally void of much of the needed ethical and deep moral commitment to which the Jews were called. If the black man is to be numbered among God's chosen, then there should be no doubt that he is under the same obligation as were the Jews. To be chosen calls for the same kind of responsibility. Indeed, to be different may not be the same as to be separate.

To work out new concepts of black selfhood and "set afoot a new man" without the same deep ethical commitment to which

[7] Frantz Fanon, *The Wretched of the Earth* (New York: Grove Press, 1966), p. 255.

the Jews were called in the Old Testament is totally inadequate for any chosen people. This is especially true for the current black man. Nothing short of such a deep commitment is adequate for liberation. To be liberated is to be ethically different.

To carry the example further, it must be recalled that the Jew was to make no covenant with any other nation (Exod. 23:32; 34:12-15). Intermarriage with persons of other nations was absolutely forbidden (Exod. 34:16). In Old Testament times, holiness had to be protected. Nothing—absolutely nothing—was allowed to taint the purity of Israel. Purity and holiness had to be protected, even if it meant the total extermination of the enemies —not as the enemies of Israel, but rather as the enemies of the holiness of God. At that time, the Jews knew no other way. There was nothing evil in this mandate; it was merely a passion for holiness; it held a note of survival. There was nothing political in the mandate, there was no thought of a master race who was to exterminate other people in the name of the master race; it was the holiness of God alone that mattered.

Indeed, William Barclay is right when he contends that "the day had not yet come—it was to come—when they began to see that the best way to destroy God's enemies is not to kill them but, rather, to make them God's friends; God's enemies are to be destroyed by converting them, not by annihilating them."[8] But that insight was to come later in Israel's history. At this point in Old Testament history, the passion for holiness produced the demand for destruction.

Jewish law combined the ethical and the ritual in such a way to fuse them as one in the Jewish way of life. The moral and the ceremonial are put side by side in a related way so much until, in a unique sense, the Jew was ever mindful of who he was. To do and to be, the act and the being, were one for the Jew. Had it not been for this fusing of the ethical and the ritual, the Jewish people may not have survived at all. Indeed, had it been the action alone, the

[8] Barclay, *Ethics in a Permissive Society,* p. 18.

46

Jew would have been no different from the Greek, the Roman, or some other good person. What made the Jew stand out, what made him different, was his ceremonial law. You can tell a Jew by what he eats and what he does not eat. The Jew, because of his religion and his sense of the ethical, was a different person. For the Jew—all honor to him—is the man who has traditionally had the courage to be different. To be separated is not the same as being different. To be different means to stand apart in an ethical sense. In the context of Old Testament ethics, many things should be noted as general characteristics. Here extensive treatment is given to what it means to be different because there is a tendency to confuse it with the concept of separation.

First of all, Old Testament ethics offer a reward in direct relation to one's obedience to God. Given obedience to God, the rains will fall and the harvest will be sure, and there will be victory over the nation's or people's enemies; and given disobedience to God, the national life will fall apart (Lev. 5:18; 19; 26; Deut. 7:12-16; 11:13-17; 28). So it is with a people who are not obedient to God's ethical mandates.

Secondly, the prophets set forth in word and deed the moral tone of their culture. The demand of the prophet was: "All right! you have had the vision, what are you going to do about it?"[9] One who has seen must be and must become by doing the will of God.

For the Old Testament Jew, the religious and the moral were so closely related that one could not separate the nonreligious from the religious. Service to fellowman was a part of the total religion of the Jewish people. "What does God want?" the prophet asks; and the answer is not church services, but is to share your bread with the poor, to take the homeless into your house, and to feed the naked. To be just and to love mercy is the mandate of the God of the Old Testament (Isa. 1:12-17; 58:8-12; Jer. 7:8-10; Amos 5:21-24). So, Judaism insisted, as does Christianity, that there

[9] Cf. *ibid.*, p. 22.

can be no religion without ethics. And to serve God cannot be separated from the mandate to serve one's fellowman. All Christians, black and white, have voiced such a view, but neither have taken it as seriously as they should.

It is conclusive that the first and highest characteristic of Old Testament ethics is its comprehensiveness. There is no aspect of life that does not fall within the scope of the ethical.

Secondly, Old Testament ethics can be characterized by its reverence for the family. This can be seen in the place given the parents.

Thirdly, the Old Testament ethic gives a central place for the dependent members of society. It gave strong protection for the widow, the fatherless, and the poor, for they were held to be very dear to God. (Deut. 10:18; 1:17; 16:19; Lev. 17:15.) But, as Barclay reminded us of the special thing about the ethics of the Old Testament:

> The Jews insisted that there must be one law for everyone, the same for the Jew and the resident alien within their gates (Lev. 24:22). There are two things about a Jew which together make an amazing paradox. The Jew never forgets he is one of the chosen people; he will not intermingle with the Gentile; but at the same time no nation ever more firmly banished racism from their society. No matter who a man was, justice was his, because God cares for him.[10]

It is interesting to note that some Old Testament scholars may not read the Jewish law as Barclay does, and they contend that it did not apply to those who were not Jewish.

In closing this section dealing with Old Testament ethics, it is helpful to remember that to the Jews ethic and business morality were of supreme importance. They even included the obligation to have fair and just weights and measures. Though many Jews of our time may no longer adhere to it, such a requirement is related

[10] *Ibid.*, pp. 23-24.

no fewer than seven times (Lev. 19:35; Deut. 25:13-16; Prov. 16:11; Ezek. 45:10-12; Amos 8:4-6; Mic. 6:10, 11). As the writer of the book of Proverbs has put it: ''A just balance and scales are the Lord's; all the weights in the bag are his work'' (Prov. 16:11).

Here the ethics of the Old Testament comes to an even sharper focus in the forthright demand that to be a chosen people is to be a responsible people. Everyone should be held responsible for what he does. A person should not only be held responsible for what he does, he should also be held responsible for the wrong he might have prevented and the damages resulting from his carelessness and thoughtlessness. There is no escape from obligation for any chosen people of God.

There is no question but that one is his brother's keeper; the Jewish religious tradition affirms that fact, reminding one over and over again that he is not only responsible for the harm he has done another, but equally responsible for the harm he could have prevented.

Finally, there is in Jewish Old Testament traditional ethics a kindness that gives one a greater understanding of what kindness should mean. Barclay says that ''the law cared because God cared.'' Old Testament ethics had its severeness at the same time it had its serenity; but it also, not quite to the degree that Barclay states it, had its mercy, its kindness, and its love. In this true sense, it is the very basis of the Christian ethic; and the Christian ethic could not have had a greater base or a finer cradle than that found in the Old Testament.

We have seen then according to Old Testament ethics that to be chosen means more than a mere thought or the satisfaction of being different; being chosen means something much deeper than the mere separatism of the black community would imply. To be chosen means that God has placed upon the people, be they Jewish, black, or white, a greater responsibility. This should not precipitate their considering themselves better than others; it is an

49

obligation of accepting an awareness that although much is given, much more is to be expected.

To be chosen, above all else, is to be obedient. No chosen people have ever been exempt from obedience to some external standards of conduct, to some external objective law or mandate of the God who does the choosing. When one looks at the long mutual struggle of both the black and the white races as they have struggled upward from the low level of slavery, one can but recognize the different ethical mandate for each. Both peoples must take more seriously the ethical mandates of this hour in history.

To be a chosen people, in some ethical sense, means to be worthy of the one who has chosen you to be his own; to act as he would have you act. In this Christian sense, and in the Old Testament sense, God required then as he requires now an ethical response; they must now, as they always have, accept their responsibility by acting as chosen people. To be chosen may well mean little more than to believe that one has been chosen and to act accordingly. The thought that one is, indeed, chosen makes all the difference in the world—if one takes the mandate seriously. To be chosen by God is to accept a larger ethical mandate.

One can never suggest, of course, that there were not more concrete reasons for the traditional Jewish sense of chosenness. Indeed, the idea of being chosen could have been supported by far fewer facts than those supporting the Jewish claim. In this context, it is quite enough to make that point in relation to Old Testament ethics. However, some more extensive consideration will be given to the concept of being chosen as it might relate to black people in a later chapter.

To lay the groundwork for a black Christian ethics, some further consideration should be given to the New Testament ethical tradition as might be related to the teachings of Jesus and Paul. We turn now to the New Testament roots of black Christian ethics.

## New Testament Roots of Black Christian Ethics

*Christian Ethics in the Teachings of Jesus*

Many black and white people are currently asking if Jesus has anything to do with today's ethical issues. Black people are especially skeptical as to whether the New Testament Christian ethic is relevant for many of the current problems of our times; they are much more critical of the inability of the Christian ethic to make a radical difference in the black man's current struggle against white racism. Indeed, one is subjected on every side to strong theoretical arguments that neither Old nor New Testament ethics are related to some of the most current and persistent ills of today. Many ask how the teachings of past periods can have any relevance for today. How can the one called Jesus Christ, whose travels were limited to the tiny country of Palestine, about one hundred and fifty miles long and about forty-five miles from east to west, conceive and espouse an ethic that would be adequate for the complex problems which now extend even beyond this world into outer space? How could Jesus Christ, reared in the simple culture of isolated Palestine, transmit to us an ethic that is adequate for the many complex problems of the current modern world? Others might further ask if Jesus, who never traveled more than seventy miles from his home, has anything to say to an American whose summer holiday in faraway Africa is commonplace and for whom a flight to the moon is a real possibility? So the question basically is how can the teachings of Jesus have any connections and relevancy for today's current issues?

William Barclay's *Ethics in a Permissive Society* offers two suggestions for those who would tend to contend that Jesus has nothing to say for today:

> Externals can change while the underlying principles remain the same. Take the case of buildings. There is a very great difference between the Pyramids in Egypt, the Parthenon in Athens, Canterbury Cathedral, . . . and the Post Office Tower in London. Externally, they

51

look worlds apart, and yet underlying them all there are the same laws of architecture, because if there were not, they would simply fall down. The externals can be as different as can be; the underlying principle is the same.

Now add the second thing. The one thing that the Christian ethic is all about is personal relationships. It is about the relationship between men and men, and men and women, and men and women and God; and personal relationships don't change. Love and hate, honor and loyalty remain the same.[11]

These words by Barclay remind us that the ethics of the New Testament and the Bible, as a whole, are as valid today as they ever were, assuming that one understands the meaning and application of the ethical mandates. The ethical teachings of Jesus are related to unchangeable things. Relations will not alter as long as men are men, women are women, and God is God.

One may well ask what does the Christian faith, with its seeming inability to deal adequately with the problem of racism, have to do with the current politics of liberation. What can Jesus say to the black man in his struggle for freedom and full recognition within the context of pro-white American culture? The answer is quite simple. Christian ethics are directly related to community. It is an ethic which if fully embraced would make it impossible for a person, white or black, to refuse to come to grips with his fellowman. The Christian ethic is all about relationships involving love, loyalty, forgiveness, and service. There are ethical relations which can only be found in community and can only be fully exercised within the human context of community.

If one approaches Christian ethics with any degree of seriousness, he comes eventually to the question of what is to be considered the unique character of New Testament ethics. What is it that characterizes the personal relationship of the Christian with his fellowmen?

The quality of that relationship between man and man can only

---

[11] *Ibid.*, p. 29.

be answered by moving one step further to ask what are the personal relationships of God with his creatures as were taught by Jesus? The answers to this question are simple, if we are under obligation to use the teachings of Jesus as a norm, because the main features of the Christian ethic lie in the demand for imitation. Men are to imitate Jesus. Peter reminds us that Jesus left "an example, that you should follow in his steps" (I Pet. 2:21). Christians are to copy the life and teachings of Jesus. In Paul's teachings, as will be discussed later, the demand is to imitate God as he was exampled in Jesus Christ. This is a reasonable demand since man, black or white, as the Bible would put it, is made in the image and the likeness of God himself (Gen. 1:26, 27; Eph. 5:1). What did Jesus say about God that was so new; what did he tell them that was so different about God's personal relationships with his people?

Such questions become all the more important for the black man, especially when one talks about the Christian ethic and what it means to the politics of liberation. First of all, if we relate God to the black man's struggle for liberation and ultimate freedom, we must relate him in such a way as not to make him less than the God who was revealed in the person, life, and teachings of Jesus. One possible misunderstanding of God in relation to man is to be found in the Greek understanding of God. The Greek idea of God, in its basic sense, is that God relates to man in absolute serenity; a serenity which nothing on earth or nothing in heaven can alter or affect. In this basic idea, there is the contention that the one essential thing about God's nature and being was this serene, undisturbed, absolute, and untouchable peace. To have that peace, according to the Greek views, God had to be totally without feeling. Man was to relate to God in this totally impersonal sense.

The Christian understanding of God, as it was revealed in the life and teachings of Jesus, is that God cares desperately what happens to man. God is directly involved in the human situation;

53

he is afflicted in all of our afflictions. Above all, he is a God who cares and who is deeply concerned. Indeed, God so loved the world, and in so loving the world, he was concerned with the plight of those people. The Christian ethic is an ethic of concern. The mandate of the Christian ethic is whether or not you were concerned about people in their joys *and* in their troubles? One cannot fulfill the mandate of the Christian ethic and not care when he sees need, when he sees people starving, when he sees people half-naked, when he sees people overburdened with labor. There must be a feeling of obligation, there must be a deep compulsion to care about the human condition.

The basis of the Christian ethic is the basis of the Being of God, the meaning of the life of Jesus Christ for us is concern. Concern for others was alien to the Greeks, who saw life only in terms of a God who was serene, isolated, untouched, freed from all of the feelings and emotions which Jesus revealed as being basic to the nature and being of the God of the Christian faith. To the contrary, to be like God, according to Greek thought, one had to "teach one's self not to care."[12]

The Stoics of old went further than did the Greeks; they saw life as a process of learning not to care. It was an educative process for them. In his advice, Epictetus taught those who followed his teachings how to learn not to care. Begin, he says, with a torn robe or a broken cup or plate and tell yourself that you don't care. Go on to the death of a pet dog or horse and say the same. In the end you will come to a stage when you can stand beside the bed of a loved one and see that loved one die, and not care. For the Stoics, life was an educative process of not caring; for the Christian, life is a process of learning to care—like God.

The New Testament translates this concerned attitude into a higher ethics of love, and since this is at the very heart of the Christian ethic, a closer look would help to make it more intelligible within this context. An understanding of the love ethics will

[12] *Ibid.*, p. 31.

be especially helpful if we are to relate the black man's struggle to God. For liberation to be fully understood, we must understand the full meaning of the kind of love to which Jesus called those who would imitate him as an example of how persons ought to care for each other. In any sense, love must be a norm as we relate to other people, especially as we relate to the unlovable. What is this love ethic to which Jesus called those who would be his followers? For one to be liberated from the oppressor, his actions must not be conditioned by the actions of the oppressor toward him.

The Greeks had several words for love: (a) they knew all about the love which was expressed in mere passion and desire, over-mastering in its intensity; they called that kind of love *eros;* (b) they knew fully the steadfast love of a deep affection which comes from the mutual experience of facing life together; indeed, they were fully understanding of the lasting love which binds two people together, even when passion is spent; they called that love *philia;* (c) the Greeks knew of the love which a child has for his parent, a son for his mother, a daughter for her father, and a brother for his sister; a love which sex does not enter at all; they called it *storge.* (d) but the love which Jesus demands is none of these types; it is *agapé.* What is it, this agapé? Jesus said something of it in his Sermon on the Mount. Hear his words on the attitude of God toward man:

> You have heard that it was said, "You shall love your neighbor, and hate your enemy." But I say to you, Love your enemies and pray for those who persecute you, so that you may be sons of your Father, who is in Heaven; for he makes his sun rise on the evil and on the good, and sends rain on the just and the unjust. (Matt. 5:43-45)

As an example for those who are oppressed, for those who would call some men good and other men bad, for those who would seek revenge for the evils done them, Jesus is saying to the good and the evil, to the just and the unjust, "God gives his gifts equally to both." Indeed, it means that whether a person is good or bad, God's good will goes out to him; God wants nothing but his good; God's benevolence is around him and above him. God may well not love what he *does,* but because he does unloving things has nothing to do with God's attitude toward him as a person.

This is what Christian love is. It is an attitude toward other people, be they good people or bad people. It is, as Barclay would put it, the attitude of goodwill that cannot be altered, the desire for man's good cannot be killed. It is obvious that this kind of attitude toward people is not simply a shallow response of the heart; it is more than an emotional reaction; it is, rather, an act of the will. It is not simply the heart that goes out to another; it is, rather, the whole being. This is what equates such a response with the moral imperative. Immanuel Kant put it well, in quite another context, when he reminded us:

> It is in this way, undoubtedly, that we should understand those passages of Scripture which command us to love our neighbor and even our enemy. For love, as an inclination, cannot be commanded. But kindness done from duty, also when no inclination impels it, and even when it is opposed by a natural and unconquerable aversion, is practical love, not pathological love. It resides in the will and not in feeling, in principles of action and not in tender sympathy; and it alone can be commanded.[13]

It would be impossible to demand that one should merely love his enemy; however, it is possible to contend that one must try to be like God. In doing so, one is compelled never to wish anything but good for others. One who is under such an obligation will look at every person with the eyes that are like God's eyes; with the eyes of goodwill.

In talking about the love of God, Martin Luther rightly contended that sinners are attractive because they are loved, not loved

---

[13] Immanuel Kant, *The Moral Law or Kant's Groundwork of the Metaphysics of Morals,* trans. by H. J. Paton (London: Hutchinson's University Library, 1947), p. 7.

because they are attractive. God does not love a person because he is attractive, he loves the person as he is; and by his love, he recreates persons and remakes them so they are fit for his love. This is how one should love others. It may be that God loves us for what we should be rather than for what we are. The strange thing about Christian love is that it has about it that attitude of the mind, of the will, and of the whole being which can create the will and the power to love the unlovely, the unloveable, the unloving—even those who hate us, hurt us, and injure us. This is the higher mandate of love. In the sense that they do to us what they like, we will do them only good; we will never have anything but goodwill toward them, and we will never seek anything but their good. Such a love is one that

> has learned to look on men as God looks on them, with an eye which is not blind to their faults and their failings and their sins, but which for ever and for ever yearns to help, and the worse the man is, the greater the yearning to help. There is a sense in which the more a man hurts me the more I must love him, because the more he needs my love.[14]

If it is true that we agree with Martin Luther, then we can say with him that the love of God does not seek to find, but through love it seems to create that which is pleasing to it; and that while human love tends to love only that which is loveable, divine love loves that which is unloveable, and by loving that which is unlovable, it makes it loveable.

The Christian love, to be like God's love, has to have this attitude of unchanging good will, but it does not simply accept people as they are, as if it did not matter if they always remained so. The Christian's love, like God's love, has to be ever active, progressive, and forward. It must, as does God's love, employ strategy; it must, as does God's love, have a positive action on behalf of the one loved, in a never-ending attempt to make him or

[14] Barclay, *Ethics in a Permissive Society*, p. 35.

her loveable. Unchanging love never gives up. The Christian ethic, in this sense, is a positive ethic. That is to say the Christian ethic tells us what we should do rather than what we should not do. The Christian ethic turns the Golden Rule around, and the thou shall nots become thou shalls. The Matthew 7:12 version of the Golden Rule is: "So whatever you wish that men would do to you, do so to them." The Christian demand, then, is not simply that we abstain from doing things to others, but its central demand is that we actively do to them what we would wish them do to us.

It must be concluded that the Christian love ethic is a total ethic of thought as well as an ethic of action, of feeling as well as of conduct. But one must take even greater care how he states this inner demand of ethics on the human spirit, and more particular care should be given one's understanding of its meaning as a principle for black Christian ethics.

In looking at the Christian ethics in the teachings of Jesus, a black person may be led to feel that it is unreal and, thus, not applicable to the problems of the black man's liberation struggle. Especially is this true if one reads the ethics of Jesus with less than a full grasp of what Jesus is trying to say, even to the man who is considered the slave. There are a few general reasons why this is true. First of all, the ethics of Jesus is a call to a high mark of action, and it therefore calls for a love that is much higher than our mere expressions of human love. Dr. Daniel Day Williams rightly reminds us that: "the deepest mystery of love is not simply the power of self-denial, but the capacity in every love to learn self-giving and thus within the vital impulses of creaturely existence to prepare for the claim of God upon the spirit." [15]

Therefore to love the enemy is not alien to human love, if human love is related to the higher expressions of God's love. Agapé offers a claim on human love because it transcends every private satisfaction, desire, or value. Agapé involves the transpos-

[15] Daniel Day Williams, *The Spirit and the Forms of Love* (New York: Harper & Row, 1968), pp. 210-11.

ing of life so that every human love participates in a love greater than self.

Secondly, black Christian ethics can, as does the broader discipline of the ethics of Jesus, do no less than call the black Christian to an ever higher expression of human love. Christian ethics, from the black perspective, can be threatening and painful in what it demands of black selfhood and its present forms of good. The authentic claims of Christian ethics, as seen in the teachings of Jesus, break open every present form for the sake of the new. Indeed, it is always a call to a more complete and inclusive community of meaning.

Black theology, as has been said before with few exceptions, has been conceived and written from a somewhat limited adherence to Christian ethical principles. If Christian principles are directly related to black theology at all, they are related in a rather narrow and selective way, and for the most part, they are related only to those passages of Scripture which fit some of the narrow themes of current black theology—such as liberation, freedom, and the black man's struggle for status within the context of American culture. There is far too little attention given to means; there is, rather, often too much attention given to the mere end results of actions viewed as authentic liberation struggle. The act and the being are too often so separated that one would think that it matters not what avenue the slave or the oppressed black man may take to freedom—he will arrive there, whole in person, self, and soul. Agapé, in the more mature understanding of personhood, may well further threaten the basic assumptions of some black Christians who would point to a too narrow Christian way to liberation; for agapé cannot be conceived as just another love added to all other human expressions, neither is it to be conceived as a mere contradiction; it is, rather, an expression which underlies all other expressions, leading them, as it were, toward the discovery of their own limits, thus releasing a new possibility in the self that was meant for a much higher communion. Indeed:

God disclosed himself as agapé. We do not discover his love welling up within us. We discover it as the boundary of our existence, in the experience of crisis, and in the overwhelming goodness for which we give thanks, or at the abyss of despair toward which we plunge. Agapé is the affirmation of life, the forgiveness of sin, the spirit in which the self can give itself away and yet be fulfilled.[16]

Void of the God element, no human love can redirect itself by its own power toward that which transcends much of the human climate that is dehumanizing and bad. Human understanding is too often lost in the darkness of evil; it is much too often twisted with hatred or mere self-seeking interest. Indeed, is this not why so much of the early black power literature which ought to have been calling the black man to higher ethical acts of self-sacrifice was calling him rather to little more than vengeful attacks on others?

Mankind; black or white, has a deep need to belong, to be secure in relationship to the other, to find the self fulfilled and loved. It is also true that this deep need to belong is so great that when it is blocked, as has been the case with both the black and the white man within the context of a pro-white society, the will to love expresses itself in the demonic passion of fanaticism, the tendency toward self-worship, arrogance, and a feeling of superiority toward those who threaten even little securities. This is a current black-white problem, the past has allowed neither to be fulfilled. The mutual need for love, which neither have been able to escape because both are unfulfilled, has become for each a current torment, an agony; and for each it has become a source of self-destruction and represents a tendency toward violence. The white man has traditionally been free to express his torment, his hate, and his violence; the black man has just now become free enough to do so. The very law of life demands that to be a self, one has to belong to the greater society of being; the right to belong cannot be blocked by the other without the would-be

[16] *Ibid.,* p. 210.

blocker placing his own personhood in danger. This is but a part of the larger implications of the ethics of Jesus in the New Testament. As the black man increases his will to be free, we may well see larger expressions of what oppression has done to both black and white people in the past.

With these foundational lessons from the ethical teachings of Jesus, we turn now to a shorter consideration of the ethical teachings of Paul.

## Christian Ethics in the Teachings of Paul

While there are many who would still hold that the Pauline ethic is nineteen-hundred-years-old, it is still valid as ever, even though its implications are still being worked out. Yet others contend that Paul is out of date and that his teachings have been outmoded by the current demands of our time. The current black mood is to exclude Paul's teachings because of his views concerning the master-slave relations of his day.

Those who take issue with Paul probably do so with a somewhat shallow understanding of the deeper concepts of liberation and freedom. Paul and the New Testament generally use the concepts of liberation and freedom with almost a totally spiritual meaning. Little or nothing is said in the New Testament about the political emancipation of the slaves. Two things need to be clear on the subject. First of all, to have politically emancipated slaves would have produced chaos and, in the end, nothing but mass executions. Even if a political move to emancipate slaves had succeeded at that time, there was no free market for labor. The time was not ripe. Few blacks would agree with such reasoning. Secondly, when Paul sent Onesiumus back to Philemon, he sent him back no longer as a slave only, but also as a brother (Philem. 16). This is to say that Christian love and fellowship have produced a new spiritual relationship between master and slave in which these terms ceased to have any spiritual relevance at all. So much was this the case that in the congregation of the early

61

church, the master might well have found himself receiving the sacrament from the hands of the slave. Paul would have defended his teachings by contending that if men are one in Christian love, it does not matter if you call one a slave and the other master, they are brothers. There was no spiritual or physical separation. That is the ideal, and it surely was not the same as the concept of slavery in America, and it is not to be understood as the background out of which this book comes. These are, to be sure, alien concepts to the American context. To make them political or physical, as might relate to American slavery, is to misread Paul.

One must read the New Testament with a much larger understanding than the mere spiritual meaning of freedom and liberation, even if it is to be related by implication. The black Christian in America is not, as Paul would say, free from the tyranny of law; he is not free from a legalistic slavery (even now) in a political, physical, or social sense. And yet, in another sense, we must accept Paul's contention that even the slave, as a Christian, is indeed free. He is free spiritually, and yet he is bound by the fetters of responsibility and the obligation to love. He is bound by the ethics of that love to act differently from others who are not Christians and who are not controlled by ethical responsibility and who are not conditioned by such a love. However, he is also free to be a new person, and thus he is liberated and free to achieve a fuller being.

It is of interest to note further that Christian love, as Paul speaks of it, was totally unrelated to the slave-master tradition in America, especially in relation to the one sphere in which love ought to dominate and control. Ethically, love should always dominate the presentation and the defense of truth, especially in relation to other people.

As has been mentioned before, the greatest sin of the American white man was what he allowed himself to become during the period of slavery, and much of what took place happened to him as a result of his unethical presentations of truth. Bit by bit, truth was obscured by the lie of slavery, and historically we can trace the progressive attempts made by the American white man to make the institution of slavery appear to be a status ordained by God for black people. Thus, little by little, the religious defense of the lie of slavery developed into a full-blown theological justification. It is revealing to note that in the religious teachings of the white man, he attempted to convince the black man that the white man derived his right to be master directly from God. It was, for him, a divine right.

It is still more revealing to note within this context that many religionists defended slavery. (1) In general, those who defended slavery as religious apologists did so first on morally neutral grounds, contending that slavery could be whatever the master and bondsman made of it. Since it was assumed that every effort was made to evangelize the slaves, to improve their morals, to teach mercy to the master and obedience to the slave, condemnation of the institution as a whole was for many religionists unnecessary and inappropriate. (2) As these religious apologists entered a second stage, slavery was defended as sound biblically. Richard Furman, one of South Carolina's leading Baptist clergymen, contended that "the right to hold slaves is clearly established in the Holy Scriptures, both by precept and example. . . . Neither the spirit nor the letter of Scripture demands the abolition of slavery." [17] (3) A third phase in the religious apologists' defense of slavery was economic, totally outside the realm of either moral or spiritual concerns. Slaves were thought of as mere property, and laws of the transfer, use, and disposal of property were matters of civil, not ecclesiastical, jurisdiction. The slave was a thing before he was a person; thus, property rights loomed larger than human rights. Slaves were bartered, deeded, auctioned, mortgaged. They were prizes to be given away in contests, stakes to be won or lost in gambling. The market price of slaves, which

[17] Edwin Scott Gaustad, *A Religious History of America* (New York: Harper & Row, 1966), pp. 186-88.

fluctuated along with that of cotton and tobacco, was discussed in similar terms. While not all churchmen wholly accepted these views, the culture they defended did. (4) Most agreeable to religionists was the final defense of slavery as a positive good. Shifting from the argument based on the slave as property, many religious leaders later acknowledged the slave as a person. Slavery, they then argued, was a boon to the master and bondsman alike. Providence ordained slavery for the greatest good, argued theologian James Thornwell of Columbia Theological Seminary. "It has been a link in the wondrous chain of Providence. . . . The general operation of the system is kindly and benevolent; it is a real and effective discipline, and without it we are profoundly persuaded that the African race in the midst of us can never be elevated in the scale of being."[18]

> The interesting thing was that when there was no strong argument for the moral rightness of slavery, the ecclesiastical institution loomed higher than moral concern. A large segment of institutional Christianity supported slavery because it was to its advantage to do so; yet, there was always a large segment of the church that never accepted slavery, and had it not been for this segment of people, black and white, the independent moral conscience of the nation would have died.[19]

While St. Paul's teachings cannot be used to justify what came to be known as slavery in America and while his teachings cannot be directly related to the slave-master concept, as we know it, Paul's teachings are related to the problem in that they do have some current things to say to the slave as he faces his master as a person.

Though we will come back again and again to the slave and how he ought to act under the mandate of Christian love, it will suffice to point out, within this context, that the slave, if he is

[18] *Ibid.*, p. 188.

[19] Major J. Jones, *Black Awareness: A Theology of Hope* (Nashville: Abingdon Press, 1971), p. 36.

Christian, will act as a Christian in his struggle to liberate himself from the master. But even in the process of the struggle, his actions will be actions taken under the mandate of love. Means, dictated by love, will matter more than mere ends.

Paul's ethic of personal relationships is always a reciprocal ethic, and from it can be derived guidelines for the reciprocal emancipation of both the master and the slave. Master and slave both must be Christian for Paul; both have a mutual obligation. It is of this obligation that we now turn to see what it is that they both must do—if there is no longer to be a slave-master climate. However, it must be clear that Paul's teachings on love are not, and cannot be, related to American slavery because they would leave the slave a slave and the master a master. His solution was spiritual, not political or social.

# IV.
# The Ethical Problem of Being Black Under God

## Blackness Under God

If the religious black man is required to relate his concept of God to his historical existential situation in such a way as to engage God in related acts of liberation, he has several basic ethical problems. His greatest problem is to translate his faith in this God into some ordered patterns which will make God's activities in the world meaningful and intelligible. Thus, the black man's first problem is with his concept of God as an ontological being—an ontological entity quite apart from his own individual selfhood as a being. How, and in what sense, he conceives God's being will determine to a great degree how he conceives his own ontological selfhood as a being under God.

Secondly, how the black man sees himself is dependent on how he sees God. If God does not exist, then the black man's view of selfhood falls far short of being adequate. Ethically speaking, how can a man be good without God? For whom will he be good? To whom will he be thankful? To whom will he sing hymns? To know God, it would seem, is to know one's self in relation to one's knowledge of God.

The third problem which the black man faces by being black under God is the problem of knowing what God's message is for his life in relation to his ethical obligations to himself, others, and ultimately to God.

Finally, what a man conceives himself to be and the message of God for his existential situation are special problems of a unique ethical imperative for black people. For every black person, there is a sense of what he should do as a black person. All men are addressed by God as they are and where they are. God's word for every person, or people, must be understood and appropriated in the light of that understanding. God's relation to the moral imperative and the ethical incentive can only be understood in relation to one's concept of God. For black people the sense of "What ought I to do?" is unique under God.

## Blackness and God as "Holy Being"

The essential question for the average black person within the context of a pro-white society is not does God exist? It is, rather, the much deeper question: Does God care? However hard one may try, he comes back to the fact that God is a being which must be conceived as an ontological entity that is the ultimate of all being. God is, and must always be the "Holy Being," which transcends any anthropomorphic elements which may be assigned to him by man—even in attempts to make him more intelligible and relevant to an existential context or a special condition. It is necessary to speak of God ontologically within this context,

67

because there are abroad in the world, and especially in the black community, many alien concepts that challenge a clear understanding of the idea of God as a Holy Being. The concept of God, according to John Macquarrie, has a twofold meaning: "An ontological meaning insofar as the word denotes being, and an existential meaning, insofar as it expresses an attitude of commitment to, or faith in, being. . . . These two meanings belong together in the word 'God' and are inseparable."[1] The word God, in this pure sense of a Holy Being, expresses the true basic religious conviction. Macquarrie makes it still clearer when he points out: "The assertion that 'God exists' may be expressed in another way as meaning that being 'is' not alien or neutral over against us, but that it both demands and sustains us, so that through faith in being, we can, ourselves, advance into a fullness of being and fulfill the higher potentialities of selfhood."[2]

The concept of God as a Holy Being must be kept free of the mere human elements, even if used in an attempt to make the concept of God clearer. To equate the concept of the Holy Being of God with any lesser anthropomorphic concept, even in the name of intelligibility, is reductionism. Yet, because of his added burden of blackness, and the many restrictions placed upon him merely because of his color, the black man is currently engaged in an extensive reassessment of his Christian faith from a black religious frame of reference. Indeed, to relate this tendency to the concept of a Holy Being, some consideration needs to be given to such a tendency. This assessment is not to contend that the current tendency is bad; it is rather to say that the tendency should not become reductionistic or more confusing than that which much of black theology is now so critical.

In his book, *A Black Theology of Liberation*, Dr. James H. Cone is, as any black theologian should be, intensely interested in

---

[1] John Macquarrie, *Principles of Christian Theology* (New York: Charles Scribner's Sons, 1966), p. 110.

[2] *Ibid.*

relating black theology to the black man's liberation struggle. But he seems to do so at the expense of the integrity of God's Holy Being, for it is to confuse the issue of oppression and to distort black theology when one contends that:

> God himself must be known only as he reveals himself in his blackness. The blackness of God, and everything implied by it in a racist society, is the heart of Black Theology's doctrine of God. There is no place in Black Theology for a colorless God in a society when people suffer precisely because of their color. The black theologian must reject any conception of God which stifles Black self-determination by picturing God as a God of all people.[3]

To require such a stance for black theology is to misrepresent the black Christian religion and its current purpose and effectiveness for the black liberation struggle unless one concludes that God makes no ethical demands on black people in the liberation struggle. If God is not the God of all of the people, then he is the God of no people. If he is not the God of all creation, then no one would call him "Our Father." Indeed, can even black theology forget, as has been pointed out above, that "God maketh his sun to rise on the evil and on the good"?

When one reads much of black theology now, there is a concern that God is being placed on the side of black people only, without compromise or willingness to recognize him as being the God of the enemy as well. James Cone makes this point clearer when he asserts that:

> This is the key to Black Theology. It refuses to embrace any concept of God which makes black suffering the will of God. Black people should not accept slavery, lynching, or any form of injustice as tending to good. It is not permissible to appeal to the idea that God's will is inscrutable or that the righteous sufferer will be rewarded in heaven. If God has made the world in which black people *must* suffer, and if he is

[3] Cone, *A Black Theology of Liberation,* p. 120.

a God who rules, guides, and sanctifies the world, then he is a murderer. To be the God of black people, he must be against the oppression of black people.[4]

Dr. Cone, by overidentification or overcommitment of God, tends to give the impression that God is only on the black man's side. Is such an overidentification necessary? One would think not. However, except for this overstatement, Dr. Cone is clearly right in insisting that God is a part of the black man's struggle for liberation. Indeed, he is!

## Liberation Ethics and the New Black Man

So much has been said about liberation, yet it still needs broader clarification and definition. First of all, let it be clear that liberation is rational in that it requires that a person acquire an attitudinal "mind-set" that refuses to accept any external re-straints which would deny him or her the right of being. If Frantz Fanon is right when he reminds us that "man is human only to the extent to which he tries to impose his existence on another in order to be recognized by him,"[5] then it follows that to be liberated requires a person to assume the attitude of a liberated person, to accept no conditions of servitude imposed by other persons or external conditions. In an attitudinal ontological sense, then, to be liberated is to assert a selfhood that is reinforced by the weight of an independent self-affirmation that must be re-spected. Such an independent selfhood must accept no excep-tions. It must have the courage to be in spite of all external odds. It must have an acquired sense of being which asserts its ontologi-cal self at the growing edge of becoming. It is the will to assert oneself against all odds. A person who has acquired an attitude of

[4] Cone, *Black Theology and Black Power* (New York: The Seabury Press, 1969), pp. 124-25.

[5] Frantz Fanon, *Black Skins, White Masks* (New York: Grove Press, 1967), p. 216.

liberation will refuse to be treated as an object; he will assert his right to be because he has the inner courage to be himself. As Paul Tillich puts it: "The courage to be is the ethical act in which man affirms his being in spite of those elements of his existence which conflict with his essential self-affirmation."[6] In such an existential interpretation of being, nonbeing is understood to mean that which threatens being; it is that ever present fear of the possibility that there is at the core of one's being the weak inability to affirm and sustain one's right to exist. The courage to be, then, is the courage to affirm one's being by transcending fear of any dehumanizing forces which threaten that being. To be liberated then is to acquire an attitudinal mind-set that is capable of a strong self-affirmation that cannot be challenged by any external force which could replace such strength of personhood with a weak, reduced self-affirmation.

To be liberated is to be conscious of the real self, and once a person finds the identity of the real self, once he knows who he is, totally unrelated to what others may have falsely defined him to be, he will be a liberated and free person. He has known, at last, the truth of being a person, of being a self, and that truth has set him free. This is the liberation to which black Christian ethics calls all black people.

However, if one's independent selfhood comes into being in relation to a master, an oppressor, or a white person, then the problems of relating are different, for then neither one is a "man among men," they are both men among slaves or men among masters. To be a liberated person, white or black, is to know one's self and others; it is to recognize the self as an equal to others. It is to recognize the need for a deep mutual sharing of one another. To be a liberated person is to have and to know an identity of selfhood; it is also to recognize identities in others. To be a liberated person is surely to discover and to choose one's own

---

[6] Paul Tillich, *The Courage to Be* (New Haven, Conn.: Yale University Press, 1952), p. 3.

self-identity rather than simply to accept a conferred identity. The black man has just come into some degree of such a liberation and a degree of freedom, and his current struggle is with those who would deprive him of that primary and final responsibility. The liberated self, as a person, must be at ease, it must feel equal to, but no better than the other self or selves to which it must relate. To feel otherwise is not to be in mature relationship with the other, to feel less secure is not to be liberated or free.

## God's Ethical Demands for a Liberated Black People

To contend that God would identify with a struggle which aims at the "complete emancipation of Black people from White oppression by whatever means Black people, not God, deem necessary,"[7] seems to commit God to man's way, rather than to commit man to God's way. It is true that it can be said of the oppressor that he does not understand the conditions of the oppressed. It is also true that the oppressor is in no position to understand the methods which the oppressed should and should not use in the liberation struggle. It is further true that the logic of liberation is "always incomprehensible to the slave master."[8] From his vantage point of power, it is understandable that the master can never quite fully grasp what the slave means by dignity; the word is completely unintelligible to him.

However, can black theology contend with Dr. Cone that the search for black identity is the search for God, for God's identity is also a black identity? This is not to say that black identity is not a part of God's will; it is rather to contend that it is a rightful part, but not the only part. If God has made the goals of black people his only goals, it would be quite understandable that black theology could contend that it is necessary to begin the doctrine of God with an insistence on God's blackness. However, would it not

[7] Cone, *A Black Theology of Liberation*, pp. 33-34.
[8] *Ibid.*

then be true that black theology would also be contending that God is not a God of all the people?

Would not black theology also have to insist that God comes to us in his blackness, which is wholly unlike whiteness; and to receive his revelation, one must become black with him in order to understand and aid him in his work of liberation? Such a narrow view of God's revelation, for Dr. Cone, is God's self-disclosure to only black people in a situation of liberation. To know God is to know of his activities of liberation on behalf of only the oppressed black. For Dr. Cone it is blasphemy to say that God loves white people, unless that love is interpreted as his wrathful activity against them and everything that whiteness stands for in this society. If the wrath of God is his almighty no against the white man's yes, then black people want to know where the no of God is today in white America.[9] If one could accept Cone's view, he would still have serious questions to ask of the nature of God as Father of all peoples, and there would also be the larger question as to whether Cone's God is big enough for the liberation struggle.

## Ethical Guidelines for Liberation

First of all, it seems totally impossible to dismiss the deeper ethical obligations which the black Christian has for the ex-master, oppressor, white man. There can be no true liberation as long as it excludes the oppressor; he is the key to liberation, however it may be conceived. It is from him that one must be liberated. He has to be considered. However, the black Christian can never dismiss the fact that the white oppressor is also God's child in need of a redemption of a different kind.

Secondly, Christian love would demand no less than that the ex-slave, oppressed, black man must maintain a spirit of love which will dominate his attitude and his response toward both

[9] *Ibid.*, pp. 40, 121, 124, 132.

73

insult and injury from the oppressor. Revenge will, and must be, left to God. This seems to be so because there is no way that one can ever measure the exact amount of revenge for the equal amount of insult or injury that one has received. There is always a tendency to overdo it in repaying the enemy for the wrong he has done.

Thirdly, applied Christian love would bring the oppressor and the oppressed into a totally new relationship wherein there is a new dimension of mutual understanding, not of indifference, but of active, positive goodwill.

Finally, using love as a guideline assures that there is in every relationship a personal element that makes the relationship reciprocally binding on both parties. The love ethic never sets down an ethical right without assigning an ethical duty to it. The duty of the leader to the subordinate is every bit as clearly stated as the duty of the subordinate to the leader. They are ethically obligated to free each other. Privilege is never all on one side. Simply to possess leadership is to be involved in a responsibility for those who are led. The ethic of liberation binds all together, the ex-slave, oppressed, black man to the ex-master, oppressor, white-man—they cannot be unilaterally free in separation. No person can make a claim on any other person without at the same time recognizing a duty to the other person. The slave cannot insist on being recognized as a human being unless he also extends recognition to the master as a human being.

## The Ethical Meaning of Black Liberation

When a person is in a state of servitude, it is easy for him to accept it (or even not to notice that he is a slave), and at times it is possible for him to come to the point where he loves slavery. It would be a grave mistake to assume that all black people would freely embrace freedom or liberation were it a realizable achievement. It would be an even greater mistake to suppose that liberation, if acceptable to all, would be a simple and easy achievement. The path to liberation is not an easy path; it is taken too often by many who do not assess the cost. The path to liberation is taken most often by people who do not fully conceptualize what it means to be fully liberated; and void of a full understanding of the concept of liberation, they tend to chart the way to liberation by the use of conceptual and mental maps that are far too small.

## A. The Spiritual Meaning of Liberation

First of all, it must be understood that liberation is spiritual in one sense and political in quite another sense. There is a spiritual and a political dimension to liberation, and it is these two dimensions which are most often fused and confused to the point where neither one is a coherent separate or intelligible concept. The liberation of man is a demand, not only of nature, not only of reason, not only of society, it is above all a mandate of spirit.[10] Man is not only a spirit, he is of a much more complex nature. He is, in some sense, akin to an animal; he is also a phenomenon of the material or natural order—but above all, he is a spirit.

Spiritual liberation then can mean no less than victory over the power of what is foreign to the basic human spirit. In this victory lies the fuller meaning and conception of what it means to be a self in relation to others. But, even within a climate of victory, it is possible for man to become reenslaved. Spiritual liberation, then, is to acquire and possess the power to be a self and the security to give that self to others in a love that requires no response in kind.

The liberated one is free, or he achieves freedom, because there is within him an internalized spiritual principle, a capacity which is not determined from without. Indeed, a spiritual concentration of selfhood to which all the precepts of the spiritual pursuit summons one may well be twofold in the end. First, it may create

[10] Berdyaev, *Slavery and Freedom,* p. 247.

inner spiritual strength and independence from the many alien weaknesses which torment man. But beyond that, it may also effect a narrowing of self-consciousness; it may eventuate to a point where one is obsessed or possessed by one single idea. If such a subjective recession takes place, a mere spiritual liberation is turned into a new form of seduction and slavery. The would-be free or liberated person now becomes a self-centered, self-seeking individual who has turned within to become obsessed by an inner spirit which he should possess. Indeed, to be lost to such an inner spirit is to miss the mark of final liberation. For final liberation is possible only through a bond between the human spirit and the spirit of God, an external being which calls one ever to a spiritual liberation which is always found in a turning to a profounder depth than the inner spiritual principle in man; it is a turning to God. It calls one upward toward the objective. But there is also the danger, if the concept of God is distorted, that even a turning to God can become an idolatry born of a subjective frame of reference. A turning to the other and to God can mean no less than the turning to something beyond self within a social context and to God above. The self, the other, and God form necessary relationships for spiritual liberation and ultimate freedom.

## B. The Political Meaning of Liberation

Those who do not understand the spiritual meaning of liberation are also weak in their full grasp and understanding of the political meaning of liberation. And, yet, everyone who feels less than liberated and free is living for the future while still void of a full life. Each person who seeks liberation must define his own essence, his relation to self, to others, and to God by participating in this world; he must do so by making decisions that involve himself and all men in relation to the ultimate above. He must live with the full knowledge that man is a political being, and except for the fact that he has the freedom to participate at the level of the political, he is really not liberated or free.

The political facet of the liberation struggle is important in the sense that it necessitates participation in governmental functions such as voting, being concerned about those who hold office, and the exercise of civic responsibility. However, there are those who look at the political climate in America, the status of opportunity, social and economic conditions of the have-nots, and they do not see the possibilities for any social reform. So, they have miscon-strued current thinking in the black community to the effect that political liberation or freedom is not possible. Indeed, as one takes note of those who attempt to articulate for the majority, he may well conclude that there is little hope for social reform by peaceful means. One might cite the following reasons for such mistaken views.

First of all, there are those who have given up hope in America's ability to meet the demands of the poor and those who would share in social and political change. Indeed, too many of the rich have deep unrealistic feelings that this is as it should be. For them there is no need for any other way of life. They see the current American way of life as the only way for the simple reason that they are the persons who now receive the larger share of the economic and political advantages afforded them by the status quo. These are the people who resist any change.

Secondly, many of the current civil rights protesters and those who seek ultimate political liberation feel that there are too many people who derive benefits from the status quo to fight it success-fully. Political and social reality seem to indicate that there are very few people who now wish to overthrow the political or social systems. There seem to be still fewer people who wish to do so on purely humanitarian principles; the fact is that there are too many who would rather benefit from the system which they currently decry.

Thirdly, linked to the failure of the anarchist is the fact that they do not offer any better system of government than the one they would overthrow. They are quite honest in their refusal to make

77

elaborate blueprints of the new world they hope to create. But their disinclination to attempt specific proposals has with few exceptions led to their production of a vague and vapid vision of an idyllic society wherein the institutions of mutual aid would enable men to create a variety of cooperative relationships unimaginable in the enslaved present.

Fourthly, both individual and group efforts have too often seemed so hopeless in today's world that civil rights movements for social change—having attracted hundreds and thousands of people in the past—now find that there has been little or no change. It matters not how radical their past actions were. They have experienced the hard reality that success, whether individual or collective, is hard to come by in current society. It is discomforting to note that too many people who now join actions which do not seem to bring undue advantages to themselves will either tend to copy, maintain, or sustain the same political structures which tend to enslave them now or which enslaved the people before their own time.

Yet it matters not how hopeless the present may seem. There is no alternative for black people but to seek a more usable future. The lure of the "not-yet" of the future seems to possess each age, and it would seem that the black man of this age is no exception.

Finally, the dilemma of the future is the need for a strategy for social and political changes that are adequate for now *and* the future. Indeed, what is the strategy for sufficient social change in current American society beyond the black community, a change radical enough so that the white man and the black man can find a mutually realized ideal social order wherein there will be neither master nor slave? This is but a part of what Jürgen Moltmann calls hope and planning. He is right when he reminds us that

> without specific goals toward which hope is directed, there can be no decision about the possibilities of planning, but without planning, there can be no realistic hope.
> Both are, then, based on the idea that the reality of human life is that

history in which the existing and the possible can be fused with one another, in which the possible is realized and the new can be made possible.[11]

## C. Hope and Planning for Black Liberation

If we accept the basic scriptural premise that to know the truth is to know political liberation and freedom, it would then follow that to be liberated is a commitment to a more rational approach to all that would hinder, retard, or imperil liberation. The restrictions, the limitations, and the limiting factors which obstruct liberation and freedom must be faced with hope and planning. To change current America, black people must take the time to study the context, the enemy, his mode of action and thought. Black people must do away with conclusions that are tentative; they must seek more than victories that are partial and fragmented; they must overcome what is now fact by persistent hope and careful planning with faith that one who plans well will eventually overcome. God must become a more related part of black people's everyday assessments of where they are. Hope and planning with God means a transition to the point of laying hold on the full knowledge of what it means to be in relationship with others with whom such a prior relationship was not heretofore possible. It means also becoming knowledgeably related to even an enemy. Hope and planning can mean no less than the complete transformation of the ex-slave's attitude so that he faces the ex-master with a new stance and knowledgeably relates to him from a new and confident frame of reference.

It means being responsible in a different way and in quite a different sense. It is responsible action for a completely new and responsible life-style. Liberation means becoming a new man where one was once thought to be a mere boy. It is to be a man in such a way that others will concede it to be so.

[11] Jürgen Moltmann, *Hope and Planning* (New York: Harper & Row, 1971), p. 178 ff.

## The Fused Concepts of Liberation and Freedom

The difficulty in drawing a sharp definitional line between liberation and freedom, in any set of historical circumstances, is due to the fact that liberation and freedom are not the same, yet are closely related. Neither do those liberties which are won as a result of the many liberation struggles tell the whole and complete story of freedom. However, many of those who have struggled for both liberation and foundational freedom too often did not make the needed distinction between the two related concepts. There is nothing more confusing and futile than the attempt to fuse the concept of liberation with the concept of freedom. Liberation is a revolutionary concept; it is derived from a revolutionary struggle. Thus, it is a total of the revolutionary actions and the achievement of liberation which lead to the ultimate establishment of a broader and more stable constitutional or foundational freedom. One must keep clearly in mind that the end of rebellion is but liberation, while the end of revolution and the achievement of liberation is, or ought to be, the establishment of foundational freedom. In this same context, we must seek a further distinction between liberation and freedom. A still broader difference between the concept of freedom and the concept of liberation is needed because to use the two concepts without distinction is both confusing and misleading. Indeed, to rebel and to become part of a liberation struggle are futile actions unless they are followed by the establishment of the newly won foundational or constitutional freedom which lies beyond mere rebellion and liberation. A clearer distinction is also needed between liberation and freedom because in our current tendency to fuse the concepts, we keep forgetting that to establish freedom is a much higher and more difficult task or goal than the mere act of forcefully overthrowing the oppressor through the process of rebellion. Indeed, how often has the turmoil of the liberation struggle defeated the revolution; ultimate freedom is always but the by-product of the liberation struggle. It must be achieved beyond struggle. Moltmann is right when he reminds us: "What 'freedom' really is, is difficult to say inasmuch as we have not yet experienced the 'kingdom of freedom,' i.e., freedom in a truly free world. But, if we seek this freedom and take it to be our future, then we begin to suffer in the chains of the present." [12]

The chains of the present are the source of our current suffering, and they should always make us restless with conditions as they now are. It is this cause that should make it more urgent for black people to search for a usable definition of the concepts of liberation and broader understanding of freedom. Indeed, we seek a newer and higher view of the promise of freedom's ultimate or the concept of liberation from the age-old climate of oppression. But too often we are confused in our seeking. It may well be because we are confused in our understanding of the two concepts.

## God's Liberating Ethical Word for Black People

Black Christian ethics must deal with the givenness of revealed truth. God speaks directly to the human conditions. As has been pointed out, God speaks ethically to man in a particular historical context. Black Christian ethics must, therefore, concern itself with the context of the black experience. Black Christian ethics must relate the ethical word of God as it is revealed in the Scriptures to the plight of black Christians as they attempt to act ethically in a racist society in which the black man is victimized daily. God's revealed word must be for black people in a direct sense; it must be clear and fully intelligible as it addresses him within the context of his existential condition.

It is true that God's word is for man in general, but it is also for the black man in particular. Indeed, is there not a specific current word from God for black people? If there is a word from God for black people, it is to be expected that a God of wisdom, of justice,

[12] Moltmann, *Religion, Revolution and the Future,* p. 30.

and of love for all humans will speak wisely and lovingly to black people. What God has to say to the white, affluent oppressor surely cannot be his same word to the black, poor victims of oppression, whose main existential needs are liberation and survival. The black man who is poor, unemployed, untrained, and hopeless needs a special word from the Lord. The word of God for him must be, as Roberts says, his strength and his salvation as he lingers in his rat-infested dwelling. Indeed, there is another word from God for the oppressor, but it is a word quite different from those intended for the oppressed. Roberts contends further:

> What God unveils of his purpose to the slum dweller must be redemptive to such a man where he is first, even if it also promises deliverance, as I believe it does. . . . In the face of the reality of racism in America, the revelation of God to the Black poor is equally valid, in most cases, to the Black bourgeoisie.[13]

God's word to the black man must be both personal and social; it must be existential and political. It must be cogently concerned with both the material and the spiritual. When God speaks to man on earth, Heaven is made aware. God's word must be most meaningful and personal; it must relate always to human existence, and it must direct man towards the humanization of all facets of human life.

God's word must be a revelation to the whole man in all of his conditional relations. It must reach the black man in the depths of his personal life, but God's word is also directed to the natural context in which the black man lives. It is concerned about those environmental conditions which develop or impede his ultimate fulfillment. God's word to the despised and the rejected is aimed at restoring the dignity of those made in his likeness. "Revelation to the black man is a revelation of black power which includes

---

[13] J. Deotis Roberts, *Liberation and Reconciliation: a Black Theology* (Philadelphia: The Westminster Press, 1971) p. 80.

black awareness, Black pride, black self-respect, and a desire to determine one's own destiny."[14]

Whenever a person understands God's word in relation to his life as he is, even if he has rejected and despised himself before, he acquires a new sense of self-respect; he acquires an assurance that he is somebody, that he is indeed a child of God. From this assured relational understanding, from this new religious frame of reference comes a new sense of mission and destiny. He acts differently because he acts in relation to God and under God. As he reflects upon the word of the God of the Bible, and especially the person and the work of Christ, the black man is convinced that he is called to the same kind of fellowship as are all other men; his orders may differ as to particulars, but to follow them affords him an added sense of human dignity and equality before God.

The black man is addressed by God as he is and where he is. The voice of God sometimes calls him forth from where he is to a new place and condition. God's word always challenges him to acquire new attitudes, new perspectives, new frames of reference, and certainly a new ethical stance. Before liberation can take place, God's word to black people must be clearly heard, clearly understood, and clearly appropriated. Clear ethical and theological reflections must bring God's word and the human situation together in order that a man may be able to find himself and an ethical understanding of self in relation to God's ethical word.

To affirm the manhood of the black man, black people must affirm the goodness of creation. However, the need to affirm the goodness of creation is so strong in the black community that some religious groups have done so at the cost of rejecting a doctrine of eschatology altogether. The "pie in the sky" futuristic hope of heaven has been often abandoned totally in favor of a this-worldly, realized eschatology. Blacks, in order to believe, must be sustained by the presence and the acts of a God who is at

[14] *Ibid.*, pp. 80-81.

once benevolent and good. As a Holy Being he must be transcendent, and his word must be the ultimate standard of truth.

God's word must bespeak to the black man a kind of freedom to become what he now is not, freedom to change the course of his own life and the source of the social history of which he is a part, freedom to alter the social patterns of life that oppress and debase all human dignity and all human aspirations. If anyone would be free, he must listen and hear God's word for his own life.

# V.
# Role of the Black Church and the Black Preacher in the Liberation Struggle

## The Black Church as Liberator

When one looks at the black church and its many dimensions, it may well be true, as some would hold, that it does not lend itself to simple definitions of role or to simple conclusions as many black and white scholars would have us believe. However, many of them would agree that in too many church history sections on the black church there are either too many oversimplifications or shallow interpretations which reveal a gross lack of adequate understanding or grasp of the dynamic role which the black church has traditionally played in the black man's liberation struggle. Not to understand fully that role in the liberation struggle is to fail to understand why the black man was able to survive slavery and the subsequent years which followed. It should also be pointed out that any attempt to separate the black man's religion from his liberation struggle is to fail to see that the black church cannot be understood merely in terms of programs or structures. Indeed, Mays and Nicholson were right when they concluded that "there is in the genius of the 'soul' of the Negro church something that gives it life and vitality, that makes it stand out significantly above its buildings, creeds, rituals and doctrines, something that makes it a unique institution." [1]

However, Dr. Cone is more right when he observed:

> The black church was the creation of a black people whose daily existence was an encounter with the overwhelming and brutalizing reality of White power. For the slaves, it was the sole source of personal identity and the sense of community. Though slaves had no social, economic, or political ties as a people, they had one humiliating factor in common—serfdom! The whole of their being was engulfed in a system intent on their annihilation as persons. Their response to this overwhelming fact of their existence ranged from suicide to outright rebellion. But few slaves committed suicide. Most refused to accept the white master's definition of black humanity, and they rebelled with every ounce of humanity in them. The black church became the home base for revolution. [2]

It is quite a task for us to understand the black church and its contributions to members of the witnessing black community in the narrow sense; it is a greater task to grasp the full meaning of its even larger contributions to the black man in his struggle for liberation and freedom and in his search for black personhood. It was the black church that sustained him in his attempts to maintain a degree of religious and spiritual integrity through it all.

[1] Benjamin E. Mays and Joseph W. Nicholson, *The Negro's Church* (New York: Institute of Social and Religious Research, 1933), p. 278.

[2] Cone, *Black Theology and Black Power*, p. 92.

Bishop Joseph A. Johnson asserts that

> the church was a place where the people gathered, and there was an outpouring of souls, minds, and hearts in a devotion to God. . . . The church was a meeting place, it was a place in which the Blacks gathered to have their empty cups refilled, spirits revived, souls renewed so that they would be able to stand the onslaughts of a decadent and sick society in which they lived. Such was the character of . . . the early black church.[3]

Indeed, the black church was unique in its appropriation of the Christian faith for the simple reason that it was ordained to provide a sustaining and supporting faith for black people, and out of the life and witness of the black community before and after slavery came what might be called an enriched expression of what religion should mean in the life of a suffering and oppressed people. The black religious experience has brought human dignity to a people who were denied humanity for freedom, liberation, and personhood. Bishop Johnson rightly contends that

> to elevate and articulate the black Christian experience by white theological technicians would have inevitably resulted in the elevation and appreciation of the black Americans who produced this new interpretation of the Christian faith. It would further have meant that the black man in America would have to be glorified culturally and elevated socially and economically. The black preacher and the black community would have to be accepted on a new level. The white American cultural ego would not permit this.[4]

Whether the black church can claim all that Bishop Johnson attributes to its genius may be open to some question, but he is right in contending that white Christianity has traditionally not accepted, appreciated, recognized, or embraced even the most authentic and legitimate religious expressions of the black religi-

[3] Joseph A. Johnson, Jr., *The Soul of the Black Preacher* (New York: Pilgrim Press, 1971), p. 152.

[4] *Ibid.*, p. 153.

ous experience. Mainstream Christianity, as Joseph Washington would call it, and white theology would have been greatly informed by the religious experience of the witnessing black community.

Dr. Cone is right when he asserts that "the black churchman did not accept white interpretations of Christianity which suggested the gospel was concerned with the freedom of the soul and not the body."[5]

It was to the credit of the black church that the black man did not accept the white man's interpretations of Christianity, for control and subjection were the strong reasons for evangelizing the slaves. Religion was meant to be a means of deception and further enslavement of the body and spirit of the black man. However, contrary to the white man's intent, religious teachings created within the mind of the slave all the more desire to be free. In his religious teachings, the white man attempted to convince the black man that

> whites derived their right to rule over blacks from God. To question this right was to question the will of God and to incur divine wrath. Catechisms for the instruction of slaves in the Christian religion often contained such instructions as:
>
> Q. Who gave you a master and a mistress?
> A. God gave them to me.
> Q. Who says that you must obey them?
> A. God says that I must.[6]

It must be noted that the black churchman rejected such teachings and, rather, fixed on the liberation themes of the Bible.

Even in the time of slavery, the black church has been very much a church of this world, and it has always spoken to the issues of the times. Though one must speak more directly of the

---

[5] Cone, *Black Theology and Black Power*, p. 93.

[6] Robert Goldston, *The Negro Revolution* (New York: Macmillan, 1968), p. 70.

current historical contexts and the many issues which now face the church, it should be pointed out that traditionally the black church has been involved in the struggle for freedom and liberation. Indeed, all would have despaired had the slaves not been able to sing: "I'm So Glad that Trubbles Don't Last Always," "Soon I Will Be Done with the Trubbles of the World." A large majority of slaves refused to believe that God was irrelevant, but as they looked at this world, he appeared to offer them little hope. Therefore, to believe, to sustain his hope, the average black man had to look forward to another reality beyond time and space.

This otherworld emphasis by the black church did not mean that black people accepted the view of the white churchman that God had ordained slavery. It must also be remembered that all the spirituals and sermons were not otherworldly, as some would contend; some had as their central theme the liberation of the slave here in this world. Such spirituals as "Go Down Moses" give cogent testimony to that fact.[7]

The black church, many times an invisible institution during slavery, became visible as an institutional entity, uniting in spirit to give expression to the quest for black independence. Indeed, the black church was a means of expressing freedom.

According to Mays and Nicholson, new churches sprang up everywhere—some organized by black groups themselves, others as a result of direct expulsion from White congregations and denominations, where converted slaves had been members.[8]

Dr. Cone may well be only partly right in pointing out that

it is a credit to the humanity of Black people that they recognized their presence in White services as an adjunct of slavery. Therefore, many of them left before being expelled. For this reason, we may describe

---

[7] For a fuller and most complete understanding of the Spirituals, from a nontheological frame of reference, see John Lovell's book *"Black Song: The Forge and the Flame"* (New York: Macmillan, 1972).

[8] Cf. Mays and Nicholson, *The Negro's Church,* p. 30.

the Black churches during this period as a place of retreat from the dehumanizing forces of White power. It was one place in which the Blacks were "safe" from the new racist structures that replaced slavery. The Black church gradually became an instrument of escape instead of, as formerly, an instrument of protest.[9]

The post Civil War black church, Dr. Cone wrongly contends, lost its zeal for freedom in the midst of new structures of the post-reconstruction period. The black minister remained the spokesman for the black people, but faced with insurmountable obstacles, he succumbed to the cajolery and the bribery of the white power structure and became its foil.

One cannot agree with Dr. Cone when he further contends "that for freedom, he substituted drinking, dancing, and smoking, and this-world concerns were minimized in favor of a kingdom beyond this world. Endurance now, liberty later, was the general theme of the Black church."[10]

After such sweeping criticism of the black church and of the black minister, Dr. Cone comes back and rightly retracts or modifies his statements to concede:

In all fairness to the black church and its leaders, it should be pointed out that the apostasy of the black church is partly understandable. If they had not supported the caste system of segregation and discrimination, they would have placed their lives and the lives of their people in danger. They would have been lynched and their churches burned. Thus, by cooperating with the system, they protected their lives and the lives of their people from the menacing threat of racism. But this is not an excuse for their lack of obedience to Christ. It merely explains it.[11]

It is quite easy to say what one should have done had one's life and the life of one's whole people been at stake. A part of the

---

[9] Cone, *Black Theology and Black Power*, p. 104.

[10] *Ibid.*, p. 105.

[11] *Ibid.*, p. 107.

genius of the black church is that it carefully guided a people through a time of great struggle. To preach a full truth, not compromising at points, might well have invited genocide for the black preacher and his people. Post–Civil War times called for great caution; the climate was not nearly so permissive for black church life as in pre–Civil War times. Newly freed black men had been put in places of leadership, displacing whites. Many times they had been removed from such places by force; many times they had been killed in the process. Law and order was for the white man. The death of a slave represented a loss to the owner, but now a freed dead black man was no loss to anyone. Whether one is critical of the black church for its lack of aggressive protest or praises it for its strategy of deception may be determined by how one reads post–Civil War history.

Dr. Cone is wrong when he says:

> Indeed, it is hard to read objectively the history of the post–Civil War black church and not come to an absolute conclusion that the "real sin of the black church and its leaders is that they even convinced themselves that they were doing the right thing by advocating the obedience to white oppression as a means of entering at death the future age of heavenly bliss." [12]

The black man's religion enabled him to survive the brutalities and oppression that a white racist society inflicted upon him. In spite of all, it enabled black men to affirm themselves as members of the kingdom of God while living in a culture which looked upon them as creatures less than human. To miss this point is to misread the role of the black church in the liberation struggle.

Dr. DuBois rightly noted that it is difficult to imagine what slavery was like. "It was oppression beyond all conception; cruelty which defies description, degradation, whipping and starvation and the absolute negation of human rights." [13] Yet, in

[12] *Ibid.*, p. 107.

[13] W. E. B. DuBois, *Black Reconstruction in America* (New York: World Publishing Co., 1964), p. 8.

the midst of such oppression, black men affirmed their humanity, even though it was despised and degraded. They were able to keep such a faith alive because of the unique role which the black church played. Historical circumstances have made its role, its people, its task, and its gospel peculiar; this is a part of the uniqueness of the black church.

## The Black Preacher as Liberator

As a liberator, the historical task of the preacher has traditionally been to make intelligible—by articulate word—the fact that the black church ought to be that special part of the world that seeks out, makes known, and makes fully clear what God is doing in the world. Any black church fails if it does not clearly identify God's work in the world so that all may see and understand. The black preacher, when he is effective among his people, must be that breed of a man of God who knows firsthand how God deals with persons, and, above all, he must know what God would have him say to the current issues of his time. Such has been his traditional role; such is his current role today. Bishop Johnson, speaking of this traditional role, observes that:

> The early black preacher was primarily that preacher of the Word. His messages were determined by the reality of death, the difficulties of life, and the saving word which he discovered in the Bible. . . . The black preacher was an interpreter of the black experience. He interpreted it in the light of God's revelation in Jesus Christ, and thereby provided the moral dynamics for living.[14]

The black preacher used his calling, his insight, and his knowledge of God as means to help ease the burdens of oppression. Through the years, as has been mentioned in another context, black leadership has used this idea of a people chosen in

[14] Johnson, *The Soul of the Black Preacher*, p. 151.

somewhat the same way. And who can argue with the ideal, in reality or in fact; indeed, black people are, as all other people, a chosen people.

The historical role of the black preacher is further unique because he has traditionally ministered to a different kind of people having a different kind of experience within the context of American culture.

It was the black preacher who, more clearly than any other person of his time, articulated the aspirations of a people. The words of the Reverend Highland Garnett illustrate with what eloquence such men communicated the gospel. In 1848, at Buffalo, New York, he said:

> The humblest peasant is as free in the sight of God as the proudest monarch that ever swayed a sceptre. Liberty is a spirit sent out from God and, like its great author, is no respector of persons.
>
> Brethren, the time has come when you must act for yourselves. It is an old and true saying that if hereditary bondsmen would be free, they must, themselves, strike the blow.[15]

The black preacher, we may conclude, was the genius of the black church because he was of the people. He saw his task as seeing his people through this difficult time in history, and he preached to the slaves in such a way as not to appear to be against slavery openly (had he done so, he would have been killed along with many of his people). He was rather to make religion a means of developing not only an adequate discipline for surviving the ordeal of the Black Experience, but also a living ground of hope for the future, no matter what may have been the ordeal.

### The Black Preacher as Liberation Theologian

Many historians have contended that the black preacher was not a theologian, but to conclude such is not to have read his mes-

[15] Quoted in Benjamin E. Mays, *The Negro's God* (New York: Atheneum, 1968), p. 46.

sage. There are many examples of the black preacher as theologian, but the Reverend Nathaniel Paul gives us a clear and classic example of the content of the black theology of that time. The deep and troubling questions dealt with the theological question of what kind of God could admit the enslavement of a people in such a manner, if he is indeed the Father of all mankind. Is it any wonder that Nathaniel Paul should have asked such a deep and cogent question in his mood of musing? Hear him, as he speaks from the past:

Tell me, ye mighty waters, why did ye sustain the ponderous load of misery? Or speak, ye winds, and say why it was that ye executed your office to waft them onward to the still more dismal state; and ye proud waves, why did you not refuse to lend your aid and to have overwhelmed them with your billows? Then should they have slept sweetly in the bosom of the great deep, and so have been hid from sorrow. And, oh thou immaculate God, be not angry with us, while we come into this thy sanctuary, and make bold inquiry in this thy holy temple, why it was that thou didst look on with the calm indifference of an unconcerned spectator, when thy holy law was violated, thy divine authority despised and a portion of thine own creatures reduced to a state of mere vassalage and misery.[16]

To muse thus, to agonize thus, and then to find an answer within himself was the theological genius of the black preacher; for such must have been the thoughts of many of the early slaves and the later freed black people who looked to him for an answer to their deep agony of heart and soul. Mr. Paul gives eloquent answer in these further words of theological musing:

Hark! While he answers from on high; hear Him proclaiming from the skies—Be still, and know that I am God! Clouds and darkness are around about me, yet, righteousness and judgment are the habitation of my throne. I do my will and pleasure in the heavens above, and in the earth beneath it; it is my sovereign prerogative to bring good out of

[16] *Ibid.*, p. 46.

evil, and cause the wrath of man to praise me, and the remainder of that wrath I will restrain.[17]

Indeed, one could well equate such musing with the great passage of Scripture found in the book of Job. The questions are somewhat the same. To find a black preacher so engaged in a struggle with God is enough to establish the fact that the black preacher was an authentic theologian of his time.

To further illustrate the fact that the black preacher and the black church were not unrelated to the world in their theological outlook can be seen in their constant struggle with God over their plight as slaves. "How long, Lord?" may well have been the question on many occasions of worship. The black preacher many times was the person who uttered both the question and the answer, as in the case of Reverend Paul in the above illustration. Probably no other black preacher gave an answer quite so adequate in words as did Bishop Daniel Payne of the A. M. E. Church when he said: "With God one day is a thousand years and a thousand years as one day. Trust in him, and he will bring slavery and all of its outrages to an end. These words from the spirit world acted upon my troubled soul like water on a burning fire, and my aching heart was soothed and relieved from its burden of woes."[18]

Hope, then, for the black preacher has traditionally been a kind of restless hope and a cogent protest. On the surface it seemed patient, but it was rather a deep, restless kind of calmness that would not be stilled. This is what Moltmann means when he asserts that to have hope is not only a consolation in suffering, but also a protest of divine promise against suffering.

It is reasonable to assert and conclude that for the black Christian to be sustained in hope in the time of the great stress of slavery he had to be assured that God was fighting against slav-

[17] *Ibid.*, pp. 43 ff.
[18] *Ibid.*, p. 49

ery. The black preacher's theology assured black people that such was the case.

## The Liberation Theme in the Black Worship Experience

There are many dimensions to worship within the context of the black church. Within the black church, the approach to God is not always one of awe and expectation; it is rather, at times, one of deep questioning, deep doubt, cogent protest, thanksgiving, penitence, affirmation, participation, and celebration. Running throughout all the history of the black church have been special elements in the worship experience that are unique to the black church. This has been so because when black people gather to worship, they come out of an experience which has been uniquely their own; and the reason for their coming together was, therefore, different and peculiar. One of the central elements or dimensions in the black worship experience is celebration; and if the idea of celebration is removed as a necessary element or needed dimension, the black worship service is void of meaning, content, and intent. In relation to its social context within the black church, celebration has been something akin in meaning to the wholeness of everybody lost in the wholeness of all; it is nothing other than a divine sign in which Christ is peculiarly declared and given to all believers. They participate in the wholeness of the collective all. Celebration, within the black church then, is a kind of climate of divine-human corporateness, which is experienced by black people when they say that they have ''had church.'' It is a kind of unself-conscious participation on the part of all that prevents an analysis or an adequate definition of the experience itself. Any attempt at analyzing a black worship experience while the experience is in process is to stop celebrating. When one celebrates, he must say yes to life at a single moment when he may well have forgotten other times when life was hard and when moments were heavy and when conditions made it even impossible to celebrate. Nietzche was, perhaps, speaking of such a rare moment when he said: "If it be granted that we say yes to a single moment, then in so doing we have said yes not only to ourselves, but to all existence."[19]

The black worship experience, when it is celebration, has three important elements or ingredients: conscious excess, celebrative affirmation, and juxtaposition.

By conscious excess, it is meant that we always overdo it, and we even do so on purpose. The black worship service, when black people say they have had church, comes to a climax in such excess spiritual exuberation. Celebrative affirmation is that time when, in the moment of forgetting that to which we would ordinarily say no, we say yes to life. It includes joy in the deepest sense. It may be that time in the worship service when we affirm not that which has already taken place, but rather, that which is still only hoped for. It is in the case of the black worship service a time when there is celebration in spite of something bad or evil that has happened. The worship experience is a time when black people affirm life despite the facts of oppression, failure, and even death. This is why the slave could sing:

> Nobody knows the trouble I've seen,
> Nobody knows but Jesus.
> Nobody knows the trouble I've seen,
> Glory hallelujah!

Indeed, this was celebration in spite of the troubles that one had seen. Juxtaposition is related to the element of excess, interpreted as an essential ingredient in the black worship experience, because in the experience there is always joy as contrasted to what should and what ordinarily would be sorrow. There is always an

---

[19] Friedrich Nietzche, *The Will to Power,* trans. by Walter Kaufmann and R. J. Hollingdale (New York: Random House, 1967) as quoted in Harvey Cox, *Feast of Fools* (Cambridge: Harvard University Press, 1969), p. 22.

air or climate which is noticeably different from the everyday, the ordinary, or the common place. When the worship service reaches the point of celebration, it links those who are caught up in the experience with both the past and the future, thus helping those who worship to reach and experience affirmative dimensions of reality which they would ordinarily fear, ignore, or even deny.

There are those who have been critical of the traditional black worship experience for the simple reason that they contend that it is: superficial, that it does not recognize true reality. They contend that it stresses otherworldliness, that it ignores the present conditions or plight of the black man. However, in sharp contrast, they fail to recognize that within the black worship experience there are all the different dimensions of reality such as questioning, protest, and doubt, as well as affirmation. There is a yes to something only hoped for, something not yet a reality. To the contrary, to celebrate one needs not be a stranger to deep pain and oppression.

However, celebration is that which should not be equated with frivolity.[20] Thus, in the celebration spirit, celebration is somewhat like the painted smile on a terminally sick patient; it is a mood born not from a joyous confidence in the ultimate goodness of life, but it is derived, rather, from a despairing mood or a failure to make rational sense out of some of the dark moments of life.

## The Lost Dimension of Celebration

In looking at the Attica, New York, prison riots, one wonders if the prisoners' inability to celebrate in the midst of their condition had something to do with their choice of death over life. The Jackson brothers of California may have also come to that point. This is not to suggest adjustment. Adjustment or acceptance are far from what may be needed to endure some or most of the

[20] For a fuller explanation of celebration as festivity, see Cox, *The Feast of Fools,* pp. 21 ff.

present prison conditions, especially if one is black. It is rather to suggest that the reason many of the students of the early protest days made such an impression on the nation was that they were able to celebrate amid all of the unjust treatments. The mass meetings of those days were used as times to celebrate the victories and the defeats of each day. There were many more defeats than victories. It may be that healing will come to a large part of the black community again when more of the black people who are now caught in the grip of extreme hate are made to learn again how to celebrate, to affirm both the adversities and the high moments in current history without being suffocated by either of them. Indeed, to know only the way of hate is not to be knowledgeable of a way to survive the oppressor. Could it be that there is some connection between this lost dimension of celebration and the growing number of young black men who are taking their own lives? Attica, as bad as it was, may well be symbolic of what hate and madness can do to a person. This is not to say that such a prison should exist; it is, rather, to contend that counterhate and uncontrolled madness have never solved such conditions.

There are conditions which are always preliminary to every occasion of worship. If it is true worship, as Roger Hazelton puts it: "God becomes real as an object of truthful knowledge only insofar as he is an object of devotion at the same time, and a God who can be worshipped is as necessary to any adequate theology as a believable God is necessary to authentic worship."[21]

Then, it must also follow that the worship experience must be directed to a God considered trustworthy as the object of one's affirmation. Traditionally, contrary to what many may say, black people have always had a deep faith in a God whom they have not always fully understood; especially in the light of their suffering and servant status within the context of America's pro-white culture. Black people have, at times—like Job—called God into sharp question, but generally they have never totally abandoned

[21] Roger Hazelton, *The God We Worship* (New York: Macmillan, 1946), p.6.

their belief in him. Before the black worshiper can express anything, he must first believe that God is. Secondly, he must be impressed with what God has done, what he is doing, and what he shall or can do for and with him. Thus, the God at the center of the black worship service must be deemed worthy as an object of worship. Black people, with few exceptions, have had little trouble believing in God as a worthy object of worship. This is not to say that they have not had trouble with the distortions of the white man and even black preaching. The God of black worship as celebration must, above all, be a God deemed worthy of worship. The third consideration must deal with the questions which must precede the worship service. The worshiper must deal with the questions of why he worships? What motivates man to worship? Why does man lift an altar to God? Is it love for God because he is a worthy object, or is it because of fear? Is it, rather, for what one feels that he can derive from God, or is it for the love of God because he is God? All these questions come into focus within the black worship experience.

To reiterate, God must be a God deemed worthy of worship, and most black people worship God because they feel a deep need and dependence upon him. Faith is born of need and dependence, and when God is not presented as one who can meet this need, then the object is not to be considered worthy. Traditionally the God of the black church has been raised, not above the struggle of black people, but above the ordinary level of overidentification with mere human understanding.

# PART TWO

# VI.
# The Current Dilemma in the Black Man's Search for a Christian Social Strategy for the Politics of Liberation

## On Relating to the Enemy

The burden of relating to the white master has traditionally been a heavy one for the black man. Especially since the white master has been the one person most responsible for the traditional plight of black people in America. In facing this problem honestly the black man may well redeem the future, or he may well lose the future. Stolen from their African homes, tortured,

103

separated from family and friends, sold and resold, denied every human dignity and the right of selfhood, the black man has a reason to ask why he should be expected to do anything but hate the white man.

One of the oldest ethical problems facing mankind is the problem of what to do with the person who has injured or mistreated him. For the black man, as for every other human being, the search has been a historically difficult one.

The mandate of the second mile, the ethical requirement to love the enemy, and the admonition to turn the other cheek may well offer us the clue to how we might best solve the black-white problem in America. For, as Dr. Vincent Harding rightly asks, does not a man simply become a slave to the other man's initiative rather than his own when he feels obligated to answer his opponent merely on the opponent's terms? Is there not, perhaps, a certain kind of bondage involved when men are so anxious to keep themselves alive that they are ready to take the lives of others to prevent that occurrence?[1] Who is the master if one does not have the inner strength to go the second mile or to turn the other cheek? Perhaps, it is the abnormal thing to hate those who hate you and to do injury to the person who injures you. Indeed, is the person not stronger who has the inner strength to forgive the one who wrongs him, to love the one who hates him? Is it not true that the person who has the strength to love stands taller than the one who hates? Does it not take more strength to love the one who has wronged you, the one who has injured you? To love the one who hates you is surely not to be in bondage to the other's initiative. The slave nor the master can be free as long as they hate each other or treat each other as master and slave. As long as they do, both are what they are—merely slave and master. They are each tied to the other. One or the other or both must act differently to break the reciprocal spell that keeps them master and slave respectively.

[1] Harding, "The Religion of Black Power," *The Religious Situation*, p. 20.

As we recalled above, the whole history of the black-white question in America was confused by the early attempts of the white Christians to reduce black people to things, merely regarding them as property and not as human "others" with whom they were ethically compelled to be in covenant relationship. Here, covenant, as Paul Ramsey points out in another context is more than a contract or bargain by which an individual agrees to put himself into some measure of responsible relation with and for his fellowman, arbitrarily or accordingly as it is in his own best interest to do so. Indeed, this is a mistaken view of how human beings are related within the context of God's creation. Paul Ramsey is right when he further observes that

> a man is never without his fellow man in any such fashion, nor does he reach his neighbor only by choice or contract from which he can as easily withdraw. Instead, because his creatureliness is from the beginning in the form of fellow humanity and because the creation in him is an order to covenant, and because this means he has real being only by being *with* and *for* fellow man, we have to reckon with this in everything that is said about justice and about the rights of man. His rights have their being in, with and for covenant. The rights of man are the rights of the fellow humanity of those who bear them.[2]

To exchange humans for things is perhaps to obscure forever the insights and the sharp line of separation of which Ramsey so cogently speaks. In a covenant there can be no master-slave relation because the covenant is not a relationship with disappearing terms. It is not a pure internal relation with no irreducibly different beings to be related to each other. There is a distance in the relation, and the relatedness is in the distance. Thus, the ideal of the covenant bond stands between persons and must forever be kept.

And, yet, in quite another ethical sense, a person is a person

[2] Paul Ramsey, *Christian Ethics and the Sit-In* (New York: Association Press, 1961), p. 31.

only in saying "thou" to the otherness of the person with whom he is in covenant. One is a self only as he has acquired his very being in fellow humanity within relationship with other selves with whom he is in covenant. However, taken to its ultimate, one wonders how there can be real relations between persons without the loss of the distinctiveness of each, especially if one is a master and the other a slave. In Tillich's terms: "How can I have the courage to accomplish the movement in my existence of being apart, and simultaneously have the courage to accomplish the movement of being a part?"[3] There can never be a mutual relation between black and white people until they both come to the point where they will each recognize the fact that human rights are the rights of fellow humanity, are inalienable, and are connected with the very stuff of human nature. Within such a bond, rights must be whatever is necessary for each to have and be a self with and for each other. If one has an unalienable right, it must be a natural right to life simply because one is human. This must be so because the right to life is the single most basic precondition to human existence in covenant. In covenant, one only has freedom for self as the self is free to give itself to be for and with another; it matters not who the other is, as long as he meets the human criteria. Whether he meets such a criteria is not for one or the other to say, such has already been said by God in creation. Indeed, the source of the right to life is to be found in the fact that God summons us all into being from nothingness, into an existence in covenant as a self with others.[4]

## Humanity Beyond the Human Particulars

Ultimately man, be he slave or master, is called to an even higher relationship. Above the covenant relationship of being

[3] Tillich, *The Courage to Be,* chapters 4 and 5.

[4] Ramsey, *Christian Ethics and the Sit-In,* p. 37.

with and for the other, there is a mandate to love—which is a much more difficult order to fill. To be in covenant is to give room to the self and the other self to be in a kind of high objective relationship one to the other so that there is a yearning for the ideal good and an aspiring quest for the mutual self-realization. Indeed, there must be the selfless devotion to the good of the other, but such a covenant relation cannot be achieved without foundational love. Love, as agapé, introduces a new dimension in the relationship that was not there before in a mere covenant relation. Agape is the conditional affirmation of the other, with a complete disregard for self; it is a mutual concern for the other that commits one beyond the boundary of his own existence. Love, as was exampled in Jesus, is the empowering disposition to serve another without thought of any good that may accrue to one's self. To be loved as a self is to love the other as a self. Only by loving the other as a self can one know and experience God's ultimate love. This is the mandate of all humans, be they master or slave, for only through mutual love can they both meet the conditions of mutual redemption. This also means that one self may love another self at the level of agapé and meet the conditions for redemption, while the other self may not meet such conditions because he did not respond in love to the other who loved him. It is this commanding and demanding condition for mutuality that transforms one from the unlovable person into the lovable person. Love always makes this irresistible demand on anyone who gives himself to loving another, whether the other is lovable or unlovable. One can be in covenant without this higher dimension of love, but one cannot love without first being in covenant. However, to be an ethical incentive, James M. Gustafson has rightly suggested that love needs to be an intention, a purpose, and a norm. Gustafson further points out that by intention he is suggesting a basic direction of activity, an articulation of what such a direction is and should be; it is a purposive orientation for one's life. Gustafson also would insist that "intention suggests cognition; one has knowledge of what his intentions are, or at least he is not ignorant of them.''[5] It is here that love, given purpose, becomes a part of the moral norm needed to govern man's higher actions, even toward the enemy who has wronged him. Moral actions informed by love are governed in part by the intentions of the actors, by their thoughts about the purposes they seek to fulfill, and by the ultimate ends they seek to achieve. In this sense, the black man is an actor; he is an intending actor; he is not merely an automatic reactor to that which is totally external. If he is an ethical actor, he will then seek to act only in the direction of those goals which he believes to be worthy of achieving. He acts, if he adheres to the way of love, out of a conviction about what is good and what ought to b achieved. Thus, his ultimate motive will be to achieve a mutual understanding by means of Christian love. Such a love, in the New Testament sense, will be a love that is deeply communal. Agapé will issue or manifest itself in a relationship, even in relation to the enemy, in which the separation of the ''I'' and the ''Thou'' is overcome in a sense of oneness. To be sure, the one who loves another in this way may be unappreciated and rejected by the person loved. But the loving one still seeks to eliminate the barrier which isolates them, and he identifies his interest and purpose, his very self, with the other so that he already thinks ''we'' even while rejected.

This is not (it cannot be) a mere human love with a motive that is selfish; it is rather a selfless love without pride or arrogance. It seeks only the good for the other, because the other is the object of the concern. Whenever genuine love for the other is experienced, it brings more than an active willing and working for the other's well being; it also issues in a needed desire to share some of life's values with the other in order for him to experience the deeper joy of being for others. When love reaches its highest level of maturity in agapé, it becomes an approach to sharing God with the other. Love is, then, as Dr. L. Harold DeWolf has suggested,

[5] Gustafson, *Christ and the Moral Life,* p. 256.

"less a matter of feeling than of intention, less of glandular activity than of purpose. It is a 'set' or a state of dominant eagerness to share God's gratefully received gifts with God himself and with other persons in a community of experience."[6]

One cannot conceive that a love of any less depth could heal or again perfect the bond of brokenness that now exists between America's ex-slave and America's ex-master.

To be aware that such a healing possibility is open to both black and white Christians will require of them both the kind of openness that is suggested by Paul Lehmann when he writes that the difference between the Christian believer and the unbeliever "is defined by imaginative and behavorial sensitivity to what God is doing in the world to make and keep human life human, to achieve the maturity of men."[7] To plead for such an ultimate maturity in such a contemporary world of imperfection is to plead for no less than the way of love as was exampled in the life and teachings of Jesus Christ himself.

## The Futility of the Way of Hate

We have been reminded in the above section that love is the only way to a more human society; love, rather than hate, is the attitude which we should have toward the person who has wronged or injured us. There are many reasons why a love attitude was suggested over against an attitude of hate, retaliation, and revenge.

First of all, the agape response was suggested because of what hate can do to a person. Hate is an evil and dangerous force, and those who adhere to the way of hate subject themselves to irrepar-

[6] L. Harold DeWolf, *Responsible Freedom: Guideline for Christian Action* (New York: Harper & Row, 1971), p. 109.

[7] Paul Lehmann, *Ethics in a Christian Context* (New York: Harper & Row, 1963), p. 117.

able damage void and totally independent of any reference to others who may be the object of one's hate. Hate scars the soul and distorts the personality. Like an unchecked cancer, hate corrodes the personhood and eats away at the very stuff of being itself. Hate destroys the mind and renders it incapable of objectivity. One who hates cannot recognize beauty, and he too often tends to confuse truth with that which is false.

Secondly, love is suggested because of what hate cannot do. The late Dr. Martin Luther King, Jr., has suggested this in a moving passage.

> Returning hate for hate multiplies hate, adding deeper darkness to a night already devoid of stars. Darkness cannot drive out darkness; only light can do that. Hate cannot drive out hate; only love can do that. Hate multiplies hate, violence multiplies violence, and toughness multiplies toughness in a descending spiral of destruction.[8]

Thirdly, agapé is suggested because hate is negating; it can only destroy and dehumanize those who hate as well as those who are hated. Oglesby was right when he reminded us that: "hatred and resentment—a legitimate desire for revenge—cannot sustain a war of liberation."[9] Hate, contrary to what many would contend, is the abnormal way persons relate to each other. We were made for love because it is a positive relation which contributes a part of each person who loves to the person loved; so both find their respective humanity in the reciprocal relationship.

Fourthly, agapé is suggested because hate destroys the significance of the other, so that, as an object of hate, he cannot at the same time be a subject of worth—hence worthy of love. Hate is

[8] Martin Luther King, Jr., *Strength to Love* (New York: Harper & Row, 1959), p. 37.

[9] Barbara Deminger, "On Revolution and Equilibrium," *The Wall Within: Violence or Nonviolence in the Black Revolution* (New York: Sheed and Ward, 1971), p. 150 ff. Quoted from Richard Scaull and Carl Oglesby, *Containment and Change* (New York: Crowell-Collier, Macmillan, 1967).

the kind of relation the white man has traditionally had for the black man in America. Traditionally the black man has not been recognized, therefore, he has not been an object of love because he has not been deemed worthy. Man is human and deemed worthy of love only to the extent to which he is recognized as a being of worth as a human being and as a human person. He has only one single right: that is the ultimate right to act humanly toward the other and to demand that the other act humanly toward him. As Fanon reminds us in his *Black Skins, White Masks,* we should all do battle for the creation of a human world: that is, a world of reciprocal recognition, a world wherein every person is deemed worthy of recognition as an equal human being within the context of the human family.

Finally, agapé is suggested because becoming a self is transcending hate. To become a mature self requires full recognition of one's selfhood within the context of history. The self is, in this sense, always a becoming self, it is not a fixed entity. If the self is a becoming self, then the full meaning of personhood lies in a personal history, not in a given complete self-structure. To be a self, in this sense, is to move forever toward a fuller being. However, all being must presuppose growth toward self-realization, and all self-fulfillment is reached in relation to other selves.

Daniel Day Williams points out that there are three aspects of the growth of the self and its loves. Speaking of the love of God, which transcends human love and consummates in a kind of fulfillment of human love without completely destroying it, Dr. Williams contends first that there is in love the will to belong, which is the core of selfhood; secondly, that there is in love the discovery that belonging requires self-giving as well as receiving and the consequential search for an adequate object of love; and finally, that there is in love the dimension of hope which the self must find as an ultimate facet of love. But we learn to love in history; we learn to love within the context of or in relationship to other people. In all three of these aspects, love as agapé comes as the transforming fulfillment of the search for human love. "It is not that we discover the meaning of agapé by going into the depths of the self, but that we discover in the depths of the self a hunger born of the self's own love, which only agapé can satisfy."[10] We love others after we know God's love for us as agapé, and knowing that love directs us to love others.

To love some and not love others is only to fail to know the full meaning of God's love for us. When John Donne says no man is an island, he is not lecturing us to have consideration for others, he is stating a fact which constitutes a basic fact of our existence. Indeed, he is reminding us that we are bound together in one bundle of life.[11]

We are so made that we cannot pick whom we will or will not love. If we reject one human being, for any cause, we reject in a real sense all other human beings. "The self is thrown into an incomprehensibly vast creation, a world teeming with other creatures and other selves. Each self tries to find where it fits in this immense and threatening confusion."[12] In this context, the primordial sense of the need to belong appears. It is both a physical and a psychological need. It is the search for "at-homeness," for knowing we are and who we are as we grope for freedom to deal with our larger external world.[13]

In this struggle to become a self, Williams further points out:

There is, therefore, in all self-assertion and self-centeredness both the pole of autonomy, the affirmation of self-integrity and independence, and the pole of symboisis, which requires conformity and relatedness to the other. . . .

There is, therefore, a kind of self-giving in the most elementary level of selfhood. It is the self-giving which offers communication to the other, and craves, waits for, and is rewarded by the response of

[10] Williams, *The Spirit and Forms of Love,* p. 205.
[11] *Ibid.*
[12] *Ibid.*
[13] *Ibid.*

another. We need not endow this "self-giving" with ethical quality any more than we would the craving for food or warmth. The self must participate in being with its environment and, thus, begin to belong.[14]

Williams is suggesting that we become a self only to the degree to which we are willing to become a part of the whole. In this sense, then, to deny access to one person is to remain that much the lesser person. The self can grow only by an openness to others; it grows by overcoming fixations at any given moment of its becoming. The new self must always seek the integrity of the moment. Indeed, there can be no complete integrity void of change. In every becoming there must be some surrender of present satisfactions, defenses, and securities to a new and higher demand. The past is not rejected. The past merely gives way for a larger fulfillment and realization of personhood. The person who is not open to one person or another class of person is somewhat closed to all others. For there is in the self no separateness or independence that is apart from the other self; it is merely and must always be a part of the whole of all other persons.

## The Current Status of the Civil Rights Movement

### Black Liberation and the Black Power Slogan

One cannot assess the current status of the liberation struggle with accuracy without concluding that we have come to what might be called a post–Black Power era. This is not to say that the time for black militancy has passed, neither is it to imply that the black awareness revolution has run its course. It is, rather, to say that the age of the black power slogan, as a cliché, has gone and that much of the rhetorical language or talk must now give away to some more structured actions, hope, and planning.

Even many of those who in the Black Power era stressed separation, guerrilla warfare, revolution, and other types of vio-

[14] *Ibid.*, p. 206.

lence have come to see that there may well be better ways. But they are all rightly concluding that there is no easy way to liberation and ultimate freedom, and it remains yet to be seen clearly what other directions the civil rights struggle might take. However, it must be clearly stated that the current turbulent period in the history of America is characterized by the unyielding demands of a determined oppressed black people who have collectively come to the point where they will accept nothing less than full liberation and ultimate freedom. Their demands will not be quieted by either law and order cries, guns, or soft talk. The demands for liberation have a kind of logic of their own. The disquieting fact is that it is a logic generally misunderstood by the white oppressor.

Maybe more than anything else, or any other slogan, black power brought to the black revolution a new updated mind-set with a new and radical emphasis on blackness. Whatever new revolutionary focus in American affairs they may or may not have brought about, the new black militants of this generation in America have already sparked a profound and lasting revolution in the way black people in America see themselves. They have helped the black community succeed, as never before, in elevating the word ''black'' to such a new radical and aggressive usage that it has brought pride to many who heretofore were ill at ease when called black. The black power movement of yesterday was the first movement in America to succeed in the establishment of the word black in the vocabulary of the black man's self-expression. This has been so to the extent that the concept of blackness has become a powerful counterassertion and challenge to all of the traditional self-debasement and self-denial thoughts which the black man had of himself in the past. Indeed, such a radically new usage of blackness as a self-expression has heightened all efforts to restore to the black community a sense of a past in which they could take pride, and it has called forth a new search for some more meaningful redefinitions of links between black people in America and the black peoples of Africa. The ultimate aim of such a struggle has been to resolve the black man's thoughts concerning black-white quality; it has served to clarify this prior unclear black-white blur into some single or coherent image of himself, as a black person and as an Afro-American.

While the black power movement was an authentic facet of the civil rights struggle and while black militancy has helped establish a larger space for liberation and ultimate freedom, it still must be conceded that the black power movement has lacked the necessary programmatic thrust to move the black man into that complete ultimate status of equality and liberation. It must also be concluded that too many of the gains that are taking place now are too much the result of the prior struggle and demands of yesterday.

We may conclude that the advent of the black power concept, the urban riots, and the aversion to white sympathizers, especially within the ranks of SNCC and CORE, marked the beginning of a whole new phase of the civil rights struggle. While we agree that the black power phase of the struggle has long survived its critics and has now come to have greater relevance for the black revolution than even its authors anticipated, it still needs a more positive ethical direction.

On a still more positive side, it must be noted again that the black power concept has promoted black self-respect, black self-reliance, and black self-pride. The black power phase has seen the rise of a renewed interest in black history, black culture, and a much needed healthy pride in blackness. We may conclude then that whatever it may or may not have meant philosophically, the black power concept has changed the black community; and it has, to a large degree, changed black people in America. More than this, the black power movement has changed the black-white relationship in America so radically that conditions will never be the same as before. Since 1963, racism has become America's

115

number one domestic problem. The current black militancy movement has arisen as an expression of a new mood within the context of the black community; it has symbolized a black-white polarization that has also radically changed the goals of the civil rights movement to a new concept of what liberation ought to mean for black Americans. As has been pointed out though, it has not always fully escaped its ambiguity; it has tended also to be too weak in its programmatic emptiness and its pragmatic futility. In a real sense, the black power concept has changed the basic principles upon which the black man now seeks liberation and ultimate freedom within the context of American culture.

The following conclusions might be reached in an assessment of the current status of the civil rights movement. First of all, there can be no doubt that the concept of black power first changed the goal from integration to a kind of semi-separation, free from white help and white domination. There were those within the early days of the new movement who insisted that the black man cannot hope to be free, except as he himself gives the directions. So there was a tendency psychologically, physically, and socially to conclude that such self-determination was necessary in order for the black man to be clearer in his objectives and actions on behalf of one's own liberation and freedom.

Secondly, it must be concluded that the advent of the black power concept sought more of a political liberation and freedom with less adherence to or concern for the ethical implications of many actions that would have been ruled out of order in the prior stages of the civil rights struggle. Indeed, the new black militant was less concerned about the humanity of the enemy than were the civil rights workers before him. The humane principle of the struggle was and has since been of too little concern to him. Not being hung up on the humane principle of the struggle, he did not have to concern himself as much as did others before him about the inhuman aspects of his actions; this was why many of the new black power activities could so fully embrace the concepts of violence, revolution, and guerrilla warfare; they did not count the cost of the loss of humanity to self or to others. Liberation and freedom were their ultimate aims whatever the cost.

## The Emphasis on Black Studies in the Liberation Struggle

By embracing the concept of black power, by giving adherence to the black awareness movement, by giving themselves to a preoccupation with black history, many black people beyond the church have now come to the point of a hate frame of reference which is stifling to the human spirit. It may be that an overpreoccupation with black history, as some would say, is the root of too much of the current crisis in the black community. There are too many free black history schools within the black community. Those who have learned the importance of black history from the religion of black power may well be in danger of losing a true authentic sense of black religion or of black history. It may be that there is a tendency on the part of too many black people to overload black history with too many expectations. Too often black people who look to the current emphasis on black studies as a means of liberation or as a solution to many of the ills within the black community, may well approach black history from a totally nonscholastic frame of reference. If so, then, there is room for the deep fear that the current black studies emphasis will serve only the ideological functions of creating a mythologized concept of black history, consisting of a mere system of assertive ideas that will facilitate only the political mobilization of the black community to the exclusion of a true sense of black history. Such an ideological undertaking has tended to necessitate the substitution of a glorified version of black history for the present debased version, with neither approach being unduly concerned with the discovery of objective historical facts. Secondly, there is also room for the deep fear that the current black studies emphasis will only serve the political functions of developing and educating a group of activists who conceive of the present shallow study of

117

black history as a mere opportunity and preparation for organizational work in the black community. Thirdly, there is good reason to fear that too many black faculty members, selected to teach black history in quality educational communities, will be chosen merely on the basis of their race, ideological purity, and their political commitment and not for their academic competency.

To become critical, it would seem that black history, especially as it is being taught by many people at the black community level, and even in many quality academic communities, is not helping the black man to embrace his past with the needed joy and appreciation; it is, rather, preventing many black people from expecting or actively engaging themselves in creating a new future. Black history, for too many black people, has become a burden rather than a facilitator of the future.[15] This is not why knowledgeable black people called for the study of black history. Misconceptions should not be the purpose of black studies.

[15] See Cox, *The Feast of Fools,* p. 27 ff.

# VII.
# Toward an Adequate Methodological Christian Ethical Strategy for Liberation

Ethically speaking, during the early days of the black power movement mentioned above, many black activists such as El-dridge Cleaver, Stokley Carmichael, H. Rap Brown, and many others did not survive long because they lacked some of the deep ethical qualities needed in the civil rights struggle. To hear them speak was to sense a lack of the necessary spiritual orientation needed for a sustained and lasting leadership within the black community. They could spend hours articulating what was wrong

119

with current conditions of the black man, but actually they had too little to say about either liberation or ultimate freedom. They did not seem to know the way to liberation or to larger freedom; they seemed only able to point the way to hopelessness and despair.

Many of the black power leaders seemingly turned within and internalized their fears and hate for white people and the dark conditions linked with the affairs of this world. Within their voices there were no options, there was too much fear, hate, and too much of a deep despair, totally void of hope. Indeed, what can be more exhausting than headless submersion in everyday condtions of this world. Mere fear and despair of all sorts are but additional forms of human bondage. When a person comes to the point where he attempts to protect himself from danger by the over-statement of facts,when a person becomes too emotional to articulate his conditions based upon that truth that clearly establishes the objective realm of everyday life, he is in trouble both morally and spiritually. It must always be recalled that knowledge of truth and liberation and ultimate freedom, in any sense of the words, demand a complete victory over fear. Liberation requires the virtues of fearlessness and courage, even in the face of danger. The highest degree of fear which is experienced and overcome may become a source of knowledge. But the knowledge of truth is bestowed not by fear, but rather by victory over fear and despair. The knowledge of truth presupposes liberation and a larger freedom. Knowledge of truth which is not related to liberation and freedom is overstated, is not only a valueless truth, but is also an impossible and inadequate foundation for the future.

Liberation and foundational freedom also presuppose the existence of truth, of meaning, and of God. Liberation is the highest expression of inner security; it is unrestricted being that knows no limits except those that are self-imposed, and ultimate freedom lies beyond.

Taken in a more positive sense, as one assesses the two, the social strategies of those civil rights workers prior to the black power movement represented a more creative way of confronting the oppressor. Almost every prior civil rights campaign was based on an ethical assumption that, if anything, repression more seriously damages the soul of the oppressor than that of the oppressed. "The strategic formula, thus, included: (1) maximum arousal of a sense of injustice and discontent among the oppressed (thus, heightening and making more visible the conflict between the oppressor and the oppressed); combined with (2) strong motivation within the new base of power."[1] There is no doubt in Wogaman's mind that it is always possible for the oppressed to be on much more solid ground than the oppressor, if he keeps the moral initative.

Taken at a deeper level of thought, the current black Christian is haunted with the persistent dilemma as to whether there is this source of human good in the oppressor. But his real and more difficult ethical problem lies within himself; to make sure that he in dealing with the oppressor does not lose his own sense of the ethical and the good. Indeed, many current black Christians question whether there is or can be any hope that something good and constructive can be accomplished through the present political system. Others question whether the political system is worth the agony that it would require to reform it, if it can be reformed at all. However, the much deeper and more real question is whether or not one can even reform the current immoral political system without himself beocming immoral. This is surely the concern of most black Christians today.

Especially is this true if one comes to the point of an utter mistrust in the current political system. However, the real danger currently resides in the fact that too many black and white people have come to the point where they feel that they must go outside the system in order to achieve their ultimate goals. Wogaman puts it in focus when he reminds us:

[1] J. Philip Wogaman, "The Dilemma of Christian Social Strategy," *Toward a Discipline of Social Ethics*, pp. 188-89.

The question has both ethical and practical ramifications: Ethically, it involves the question of the legitimacy of the system involved; practically, it is a question of what, in fact, can be accomplished through the system. The dilemma occurs as the Christian strategist faces the possibility that the apparently moral forms of strategy may not be moral or that the apparently moral forms of strategy may not be effective.[2]

Indeed, most of the black Christians one meets now have acquired too little success, individually or collectively, to point to as achievements resulting from social struggle. Most black people would insist that they have already tried the way of love and nonviolence and it has not worked for them; so they are divided on the question of a feasible strategy. The question is what should be done. Which is the more effective way to achieve a better tomorrow? It is to these feasible alternatives that we now turn for some extensive assessment.

## Conflicting Concepts of Violence

### Violence as a Possible Christian Strategy for Change

The words of Jean Genet symbolize the deep despair which confronts one day by day, if he is a black person:

What ought I to do? How or by what means? Violence is but one way. Violence. If we must, let's talk about it. But, by seeing it for what it is: A word. A word used by those who elaborated and imposed the language: the masters. According to how the word will serve them, it can signify God's will; used against them, it can become a sign of shame and degradation. When white men use violence, violence is good. When black men use it, they are considered animals. However, it so happens that the blacks have exposed the tricks of the language, as they have exposed religious tricks, legal shams and social deformities. Blacks aren't afraid of words any more, regardless of the coloration the Whites might give them.

[2] *Ibid.*, p. 168.

It is evidence that recommending nonviolence to blacks is an effort to retain the Christian vocabulary which has kept them imprisoned in passivity for so long. However Christian the whites are, they don't feel guilty about using guns: that is violence. Asking blacks in America to be nonviolent means that whites are demanding a Christian virtue which they themselves do not possess. That means that whites are once again trying to dupe the blacks.[3]

These pointed words from the lips of Jean Genet bespeak the current frustration and general disenchantment which black people express toward any mention of nonviolence as either a strategy, a methodology, or even as a way of life. No serious discussion of the ideologies of violence and nonviolence could overlook the implications of the above statement. Indeed, no reflective person can deny that violence is a word subjected to many manipulations and implications not related to the ethical concerns of this book. However, no book on Christian ethics can overlook the concepts of violence and nonviolence because, as would be indicated in Miss Genet's statement above, too many people who speak of violence confine their concerns to the practical question of whether violence or nonviolence, as simple methods or strategy for social change, will work.

But what of the ethical? If it is true that "violence is [a] physical force resulting in injury or destruction of property or persons in violation of general moral belief or civil law,"[4] was the Eisenhower Commission speaking of mere strategy when they defined violence as a "behavior designed to inflict physical injury on people or damage to property," which adds the element of forethought or intention to the injurious action?[5] Colin Morris, who for a long time was in Zambia and now lives in England, speaking of mere strategy when he gave cogent expression to the nature of violence expressed in colonialism by contending that

[3] Jean Genet, in *Ramparts* (June, 1970), p. 31.

[4] George R. Edwards, *Jesus and the Politics of Violence* (New York: Harper & Row, 1972), p. 2.

[5] Hugh Davis Graham and Robert Gurr, *Violence in America,* p. xxx.

123

"to starve people is violence; to rob them of their dignity and self-respect is violence; to deny them their political rights; to discriminate against them is violence. Elaborate structures of violence make a terrorist what he is, and he faces them as the weaker adversary."[6]

There are too many definitions of violence to include within this context. Indeed, an extensive listing is not needed. However, for the sake of the current discussion, we conclude that violence is the expression of coercive powers in ways that involve physical harm to human life or personal property, or we may extend this definition to mean that "violence is physical force resulting in injury to persons or destruction of property in violation of general moral belief or civil law. It is of interest to note in the Eisenhower Commission's definition that destruction of property is listed with injury to persons within the general definitions of violence, while life in general seems to be totally excluded. When one concludes with the many definitions of violence which have no end, he is still confused to the point of agreeing with Genet in her contention that violence is just a word which defies a clear or a concise definition for the good or the evil side. Indeed, force, like violence, can be judged good or bad when one observes the myriad uses of the interchanged concepts to explain both good and bad actions. Conventional definitions are now under added strain to fix on a clear moral definition. For example, when one looks at the many definitions of violence as separate from the concepts of force, he must conclude that much that Jean Genet said of the use of the concept is true, but the question is much deeper than even her concerns would suggest, and there is need for more consideration to support or to dispel her contentions. Surely such added considerations are needed within this context because of the current attempts to fix on violence as a methodology to the exclusion of the alternative commitment,

[6] Colin Morris, *Unyoung, Uncolored, Unpoor* (Nashville: Abingdon Press, 1969), p. 96.

which many people have made to nonviolence as a way of life. We must grasp for deeper definitions of violence if we are to give the needed ethical dimensions to the discussion. What then is violence? There are according to Robert E. Fitch[7] at least three general definitions of violence. First, the classic definition of violence is that it is injury to persons or to property, as has been cited before. Secondly, violence is the use of force in excess of or apart from the end to be achieved. Within this context, it is assumed that some kind of force is necessary to achieve any end. Thirdly, violence has to do with the nature of the self. Here, the self is a human self, or it may well be conceived as a legal self created by law. Essentially, then, violence is anything that obstructs or frustrates the legitimate functioning of a person or a legal self, and it can be perpetrated without resort to either the first or second sort of violence.

One can clearly see that there are many dimensions to the definition of the concept of violence, but when one comes to the use of violence as a method for social change, then the question of its effectiveness is clearly in focus, even if no ethical questions were at all related. Assuming that it is not clearly an ethical set of criteria, one might well start the discussion by applying the theologian's theory of a just war to the use of violence as a methodology in the struggle for social change. According to these criteria, seven conditions must be met before violence could or can be conceived as a just methodology: (1) the cause fought for must itself be just; (2) the purpose of those who seek liberation must remain just while the struggles for liberation go on; (3) violence must be truly the last resort, while all other peaceful means of achieving liberation must have been exhausted; (4) the methods and measures of violence employed during the struggle to vanquish the oppressor must themselves be just; (5) the benefits which the use of violence can reasonably be expected to bring for

[7] Robert E. Fitch, "The Use of Violence," *The Christian Century* (Apr., 1968).

humanity must be greater than the evils provoked by the violent struggle itself; (6) relief must be assured for those who are in bondage; (7) the liberation and ultimate freedom achieved at the end of the struggle must be extended to all, even to those who were the prior oppressors.

There are many weaknesses in the above attempts at some jusitfications for violence. However, Jacques Ellul, in his book *Violence,* contends that there are certain laws of violence which tend to negate the above in favor of a total rejection of any violence as a method for social change. His conclusions are that it is not ethical to follow any attempt to adjudge violence as a just methodology for social change. This is not to accept Ellul's conclusions that violence is inevitable in all societies, whatever their form. It is surely not to grant that there is an inescapable law of violence, because there is room for choice at all levels of rational action, and when we deal with the ethical question, choice must be considered a prior assumption. [8]

Ellul has listed the laws of violence. The first law of violence is continuity. Once one starts using violence, he cannot get away from it because violence expresses the habit of oversimplification of situations, be they political, social, or human. Such a habit cannot very well be broken for the simple reason that once a person has begun to use violence, he will never stop using it; for, it is much more simple and practical than any other method for social change. It is simple, direct, and frequently quick. The second law of violence is reciprocity. It is true that violence creates violence, and that more violence begets and increases violence. Violence imprisons its practitioners in a cycle of action that cannot be broken by human means. All studies of violence show that violence will have but one certain result: the reciprocity and the reproduction of more violence. This will be so whether any other results are attained or not. Equal rights, legitimate defense, liberation, freedom, etc. All else are mere matters of

[8] Jacques Ellul, *Violence* (New York: The Seabury Press, 1969), pp. 93 ff.

chance; all other results, too, are subject to the reciprocity which is one of the laws of violence. According to Ellul, a third law of violence is sameness. If one assumes such a view, he must accept the great danger that there is no difference between unjustified and justified violence; violence that liberates or violence that enslaves. According to Ellul's view, every violence is identical with every other violence; this is especially true when one talks of violence against people, and here the focus is confined to violence against persons. This view accepts the fact that all violence should not be subjected to these laws, because some violence would not be applicable, but surely such sameness would be true as might relate to others, because it follows that once one chooses the way of violence, it is impossible to curb it. By the use of violence one provokes the victim of one's violence to use violence in turn, and that makes it necessary to use more violence. Once one chooses the way of violence he has also to consent in some sense to his adversary's use of violence. One cannot have his choice and demand otherwise of his adversary. A fourth law of violence is that violence begets violence, nothing else. Here one concludes, if he accepts Ellul's view, that violence has no other end. We will return to this subject later, but if we accept Ellul's view, we must conclude that violence can never realize a noble aim, can never create liberty or justice. The end does not justify the means; on the contrary, evil means corrupt good ends. So, Ellul concludes that violence will never establish a just society, and one must be impressed by his argument. Ellul's final law of violence is rationalized justification. The person who uses violence always tries to find some justification for both it and for himself. He gives some logical reason why there is no other way.

It is true, as Ellul cites in *Violence,* [9] that men of history have always had to find some justification for violence. Even black leaders, who advocate violence, do so with some elaborate attempts at rationalization. H. Rap Brown, Stokley Carmichael,

[9] *Ibid.,* pp. 103 ff.

Malcom X, and others have all given reasons which would not stand the test of ethical norms, much less the ethical criteria of love.

The one further word about violence—are there two kinds of violence? Indeed, is there a violence that liberates and a violence that enslaves? Both Ellul and Hannah Arendt[10] take the position that violence is not liberating; for the two of them, liberation or ultimate freedom can never be won by revolutionary means. However, it would seem that both Arendt and Ellul have overlooked the fact that there have been degrees of liberation achieved by revolutionary means. West Germany is better off today than it was under the Hitler regime, even though East Germany can be seen in sharp contrast. Further, it is true that Ellul nor Arendt do not understand violence from the black side when they contend that as a result of riots of the 1960s black people did not derive any positive benefits. There have been good and liberating positive changes taking place after the riots of the 60s, and there will come many more by-products of the riots of the 60s even in the 70s. But the deeper ethical question is whether we needed such violence to achieve social change or social good? How necessary is violence? Is there not a better way? Before turning to nonviolence as an alternative, there are other considerations to be met.

## Violence and the Killer Instinct

It has been interesting to follow the current debate among certain of the social science students of human nature as to the relation of violence to the question of man's basic nature. The focus of the controversy has been the book *On Aggression* by Konrad Lorenz, the Austrian expert on animal behavior who is the director of the Institute of Behavioral Physiology in Bavaria.[11]

[10] Hannah Arendt, *On Revolution* (New York: Viking Press, 1965), p. 111.
[11] Konrad Lorenz, *On Aggression* (New York: Harcourt, Brace, and World, 1966).

Lorenz contends that there is a killer instinct in man which makes him a lethal danger to himself and other members of his kind. According to Lorenz, this accounts for man's tendency toward violence under certain pathological conditions. However, Lorenz has been challenged at many points because when one looks at all of the facts, his theories do not hold up.[12] Indeed, an erroneous inference is present in any assertion which assumes that the killer instinct in man can be asserted as being directly related to its existence in animals, if indeed we can even assume the killer instinct is a universal biological fact among animals. There seem to be sufficient data to support the fact that animals do kill for food, in which case they are not vengeful or angry with their prey; but there is a qualitative difference between what is inferred by Lorenz when he refers to the so-called killer instinct in man and the relating of such a killer instinct to man's tendency toward violence.

John Paul Scott is more right when he asserts that

it can no longer be concluded that it is man's "animal nature" which is responsible for human violence in analogue with some of the aggressive animals, such as wolves, because the main source of violence between animals of the same species, as well as in humans, is social disorganization.[13]

In an article entitled, "A Constructive View of Anger, Aggression and Violence," Chris M. Meadows argues for what he calls positive and negative aggression.[14] He labels as positive aggression those actions which move a person affirmatively and asser-

[12] See M. F. Ashley Montague, ed., *Man and Aggression* (New York: Oxford University Press, 1968).

[13] John Paul Scott, "The Anatomy of Violence," *Violence in the Streets* (Chicago: Quadrangle Books, 1968), p. 65.

[14] Chris M. Meadows, "A Constructive View of Anger, Aggression and Violence," *Pastoral Psychology* (Sept. 22, 1971), pp. 9 ff.

tively forward toward some self-fulfilled goal. In negative aggression he contends that it functions physically and behaviorally in a disjunctive, "moving against," or attacking manner. Negative aggression is equivalent to the typical connotation of "aggression" in the sense that such aggression is against some other self or person. Positive aggression, Meadows further contends, includes "working through"—working through one's own psychic conflicts and identity, working through the solution to an objective problem, or working through the communication difficulties and conflicts involved in group life. Meadows asserts that, unlike negative aggression, positive aggression is involved in taking risks, self-consciously making oneself vulnerable, cutting through mistrust to establish appropriate trust.[15]

Quite unlike positive aggression, negative aggression covers a wide range of phenomena, including psychic wishes to aggress against persons or objects, specific acts of aggression, and instances of defensive aggression. Also, negative aggression includes moving against or the attack of barriers that prevent self-affirmation, constructive interpersonal relations, or creative growth toward personal wholeness. Negative aggression can either be angry aggression, or it can be instrumental, that is, without anger.

In any event, Meadows would not accept the conclusion that man is violent because he has within his nature the killer instinct which makes him a killer by nature. He agrees with Gordon W. Allport that "an individual at the beginning of his life is governed by a dependent, affiliative relationship with his mother."[16] Allport further asserts that "there is little evidence of destructive instincts in early life and that it is characterized by positive social relationships."[17]

[15] *Ibid.,* pp. 12, 13.
[16] Gordon W. Allport, *The Nature of Prejudice* (Cambridge, Mass.: Addison-Wesley Publishing Co., 1954), p. 365.
[17] *Ibid.*

130

## Anger and Violence

Closely related to violence is anger, which is sometimes included in the general definition of violence and is not assessed as separate from its relation to aggression or violence. In its most human form, "anger is the effect that mobilizes a person to protect himself against his selfhood, at all levels including injustices to or infringements against his own personal integrity or that of others, and to fight for causes, whether they be personal, group, or ideological."[18]

If such is the case, then, the question of the place of anger in the development of personhood is at stake, and it is, therefore, true as Meadows contends that "anger is built into the structure of human existence. The capacity for anger enables the human person to face and protest the threats and vulnerabilities that are intrinsic to the reality of being limited and finite, especially when he chafes under these limitations." Meadows is further right when he holds that: "Existential anger cannot be removed, but it can be confronted and accepted." However, most people in the black community have been aware for some time that there has always been a direct connection between the anger which black people have traditionally expressed toward other black people when the anger was actually anger which, under conditions of equality, they would have expressed toward white people. The black community has long sensed that anger; if it is not faced, it will turn into neurotic anger. "Neurotic anger is disproportionate to its source in the real world. Normal anger is appropriate to the situation that aroused it."[19]

To push this still further, it would seem that when the black man relates to the white man, long considered his master and oppressor, he is not free to express his true anger; however, when

[18] Chris M. Meadows, "A Constructive View of Anger, Aggression, and Violence," pp. 9 ff. (See footnote 14 on page 129.)
[19] *Ibid.*, p. 16.

he relates to his own kind, many times he expresses an anger that should have been directed at the white man. This is what Meadows calls neurotic anger or what might be referred to as misguided or disproportionate anger, which has its source in irrational or unconscious intrapsychic conflicts. Anger, which does not have its normal expression in violent actions, can be managed among equals. Indeed, there are many normal expressions of anger which are less than violent; however, when the object toward which the normal anger is to be expressed is hidden or forbidden, then intrapsychic conflicts are developed and internalized. According to this view of anger, however, such subjective conflicts do irreparable harm to the personhood. One would suppose that this view could contend that anger, suppressed, unexpressed, and sustained over a period of time may well express itself in violent actions—even against persons who were not responsible for the cause. The anger theory, if related to Freud's theory of negative aggression, fails to consider the positive aspects or benefits to be derived from the suppression of anger and more positive alternative expressions. Freud would contend that aggression arouses when the ego instincts, or the ego's struggle for self-preservation are impeded. As Freud puts it: "The ego hates, abhors, and pursues with the intent to destroy all objects which are a source of pain."[20] Aggression, for Freud in this context, is nonbiological and thus not related to sexual energy and would not be directed against one's own kind for the same reason. In this context, Freud's aggression theory is psychological, and it attempts to explain the person's reactions against threats to the personhood, either direct or indirect. Anger, for Freud, would be the result of a threat to self-fulfillment, and it would assume that violence is inevitable. Many of the black community would currently agree with Freud, but they would give a more moral justification for violence than would he. They would relate the

[20] Sigmund Freud, "Instincts and Their Vicissitudes," *Collected Papers,* VI (1915), 82.

moral justification for violence to the moral issue of what anger, resulting from any outside force obstructing the positive normal growth, development, and fulfillment of personhood. Black people contend that the person is obligated to pursue with the intent to destroy all persons who would seek to destroy them. This is self-defense, and one of the first laws of nature gives one this right. Indeed, many black people would contend, contrary to many white people who represent the object of the external threat to all black people, that threats to a person's self-esteem, obstructions within society which render them impotent, which diminish their status in their own eyes and in the eyes of others, should be met with a counterdegree of violence necessary to correct the external conditions which threaten a people's being. They would contend with more current moral concurrence that the only way to restore the black man's personal status and demonstrate power —real power—is to injure or destroy the provoking agent. A study by Megargee in 1965 revealed that overcontrolled people, as might relate to their aggressive urges, tend to explode more often in fatal violence toward or against others of his own kind. It is no small wonder that the black man tends to be more explosively violent than does his white counterpart. He is overcontrolled and restricted. The black person cannot live where he wishes, he is excluded from equal employment, his jobs are oversupervised, he is underpaid, and there are too many indirect ways which tell him that he is too much a powerless person to change those external powerful, often invisible, obstructive forces that are directed against him; thus, he strikes out at any threat or countersymbol of a threat which may not be the true locus of the threat or the center of the power. It is no wonder that much of this violence against his kind is now being redirected against whites.

## Violence and Self-Defense

Within the black community violence and anger are interrelated and cannot be completely separated, especially now that there is a realized greater degree of freedom, and black people feel more liberated than before. Though it is not articulated by the old, young black people are deep in debate concerning strategy and self-defense. There would be no deep ethical questions or theological implications were it not for the fact that those who relate self-defense to the liberation struggle also say that violence or anger are natural expressions for the physical and psychological well-being of the liberation struggle. Most current young black people would contend that not to return violence for violence is not to defend the ontological stuff of being itself. Moving the idea directly into focus, John Oliver Killens, who symbolizes such a view, contends that "men are not free until they affirm the right to defend themselves." At a much deeper level of a fuller and more conceptualized understanding of what he means by self-defense, Killens gives a more profound psychological meaning of self-defense when he states clearly that "we black folk have a deep need to defend ourselves. Indeed, we have an obligation. We must teach the brutalizers how it feels to be brutalized. We must teach them that it hurts. They'll never know unless we teach them."[21] These contentions are given deeper implications when Dr. Harding interestingly points out:

> There is, however, an even more profound issue in what Killens describes so sensitively as "a deep need" for black men to defend themselves. What he seems to be implying is this: when men have long been forced to accept the wanton attacks of their oppressors, when they have had to stand by and watch their women prostituted, it is crucial to their own sense of self-esteem that they affirm and be able to implement their affirmation of a right to strike back.
> The basic human search for a definition of manhood is here set out in significant black lineaments. Does manhood indeed depend upon the capacity to defend one's life? Is this American shiboleth really the source of freedom for men? [22]

[21] John Oliver Killens, "Symposium on Black Power," *Negro Digest,* Nov. 1966.

[22] Vincent Harding, "The Religion of Black Power," *The Religious Situation,* pp. 21-22.

134

Is self-defense the only way to true manhood and ultimate liberation? This is a question as deep as the nature of man himself. To be sure, it must not center in a mere response in kind. The book contends that the truly strong man does not have to fear, for he seeks a higher manhood, a manhood that is given example in the life of the God-man Jesus Christ, who introduced even the zealots of his time to a new and higher response. Those who adhere to black power seem unwilling even to consider the Jesus way. Indeed, can only the strong, whole man afford not to strike back—the man who has not suffered oppression, who has no need for wholeness? What of the weak person who has a need for wholeness?

To push the argument further, one must note within this context that the question of self-defense, as it is being debated in the black community today, is a sharp question for many reasons. First of all, it relates to the problem of the liberation of a people. So the question of what the lack of self-defense does to a person's basic selfhood is a serious ethical question for a black man seeking authentic self-identity. Second, the issue is not just what self-defense contributes to a person's own basic selfhood; it is also a question of how self-defense is related to liberation or foundational freedom.

Then, too, when a person contends that it is related to "the courage to be," self-defense becomes all the more an ethical question. Indeed, the question is one which deals with the basic ethical question of what he should do. It may well be that the oppressed must fully understand the deeper ethical meaning of self-defense in the light of what is really at stake here. One must raise the question as to whether the personhood of the black man is really related to self-defense.

## Violence and Liberation

When the leaders of what Dr. Harding calls the religion of black power speak of self-defense, it would seem that they speak of it individually and collectively. The emphasis in this discussion will relate to the individual for it is here that the arguments for basic self-image and self-liberation are developed. It is here that many black people are at cogent odds with the King position on the individual internalized liberating, personal strength, and the integrity of personhood to be derived from adopting nonviolence as a way of life. Their basic position can be summarized at two levels. First, externally speaking, many adherents of the black liberation movement would contend that a person must be free to defend his person against all external threats. They contend that no healthy self-esteem or ultimate sense of liberation can be developed without this basic freedom. Not to be free to defend oneself is to be saddled with a paralyzing fear, which demeans the basic stuff of personhood. This is what they would contend that Paul Tillich means by the ethical act of self-affirmation and what they would understand Frantz Fanon to mean by imposing one's existence on another. The freedom to be violent, many black people contend, is essential to a sense of liberation and healthy self-esteem. Second, internally speaking, many adherents of the black liberation movement would assert that the freedom to choose hate or love is essential; the value of each, they contend, would depend upon the response needed or called for within the context of the given moment. And here one can see the expression is from a nontheological or ethical frame of reference. Indeed, the Christian's contention that hate is demeaning is totally unacceptable. For black liberation adherents, to hate the enemy is a human reaction and is thus normal. To defend oneself against the destructive actions of the enemy is normal; any other action is abnormal and produces a weak, reduced self-affirmation. To accept the abuses of the white man, to accept his attempt not to recognize the black man's personhood, to accept his violence, external or internal, without a response in kind, black liberation adherents contend is to do the basic stuff of black personhood a disservice and thus demean it. Indeed, is Dr. Harding not right when he points out in his assessment of the mind-set of the ghetto that "as we have seen, black men have been chained to weakness for so long that any talk of voluntarily choosing a way that black community counts as weak is considered sheer madness."? [23]

It may well be true in the nonviolent approach, that the lack of self-defense, is indeed demeaning. But from an assessment of the question, it would seem that modification would have to be conceded, and such an assertion would only apply to the weak, or indeed to the person who would remain weak. It takes more strength to remain nonviolent in response to external violence from the enemy than it does to respond in kind; for, as Dr. Harding has pointed out, to respond in kind may well make the oppressor the master. Does the master not then determine what kind the response should be? Thus, to feel the need to respond to violence by becoming violent seems to make one a slave to the person or persons who called forth the act of violence as a means of self-defense. The self-defense adherents cannot escape the cogent question as to just who is the master?

Jesus was a good example. At no place did he allow the external to determine what he should say or how he should act at a given moment. Is this not what moved him to pray from the cross to forgive them? Was this not the reason he admonished Peter to put up his sword, for all those who live by the sword die by the sword? Few would suggest that Jesus was less than a person of strength.

## Nonviolence and Social Strategy

*Nonviolence and Self-Defense*

Most of the prior and current critics of the late Dr. Martin Luther King's nonviolent views were and are persons who tend to look upon his nonviolent formulations as descriptions for a mere

[23] *Ibid.*, p. 27.

methodology for social change. They do not accept his nonviolent views as a way of life as they were for Dr. King. They tend to misread his literature on the subject; they do not know of his account of an early experience of the time when his house was bombed that first time and the long agonizing hours of debating whether to take up arms and take the way of violence as a means of self-defense or to get rid of all weapons and fully embrace the way of nonviolence. He and his wife Coretta chose the latter, and for them nonviolence gradually became a way of life. Nonviolence was their only defense, and there is nothing to indicate the contrary.

Until he went to his death, nonviolence was his only defense. Many read his last statements to mean that he was moving toward a violent stance; however, if one looks at even the final literature, he must conclude that the press was attempting to make King the spokesman for the total black mood of the time, which indeed was one of violence. They pressed him for a change which he did not make.

The above are expressions meant to lead us into a deeper consideration of the way of nonviolence as a strategy for social change.

Before turning to a discussion of the larger question of social strategy, there is need for a broader discussion of Dr. King's views. Many of the current black power critics of Dr. King's way of life would contend that nonviolence as a way of life is undesirable because, as has been pointed out above, it is demeaning to the personhood of black people. They would have serious questions as to whether the nonviolent approach, as Martin Luther King put it, ''does something to the hearts and souls of those who are committed to it.'' They would question King's contention that it ''gives them 'self-respect,' '' that it calls up ''resources of strength and courage that they did not know they had.''[24]

---

[24] See Dr. King's "Pilgrimage to Nonviolence," *Christian Century* (April 13, 1960), p. 439.

Very few people will accept fully Dr. King's contention that nonviolence is not a capitulation to weakness and fear, that it demands of its advocates that difficult kind of steadfastness which can endure indignation with dignity. Fewer still, especially now, would accept Dr. King's contention that the "endurance of unearned suffering is redemptive." Neither would many others follow his contention that not only does nonviolence avoid the demeaning results that one suffers when he lends himself to external physical violence, but nonviolence also helps one avoid internal violence of the spirit. People do not accept this way of life. This is why there is such broad misreading of the literature of nonviolence and why so many people consider it less than applicable to many of the current problems of the black man's plight. It is quite true that to embrace nonviolence as a mere methodology may not contribute to the positive thrust of self-affirmation. However, to accept it as a way of life, a moral theological principle, is another matter. It is here that the nontheologians have misread Dr. King's thought; for indeed, the ultimate aim of nonviolence is not conquest, it is rather to establish a relationship. And, related to Christian love, nonviolence may well be required to avoid a motive of conquest or defeat and the need for defense of self.[25]

## Nonviolence as a Strategy for Social Change

Too often the methods of social change or strategy are not so well conceived because those who choose the way of nonviolence are not fully aware of the deep ethical consequences of their actions. Many times a whole people are committed by those who act void of an adequate assessment of the end results of what they do. Some consideration has to be given to the violent way. Now it is time to turn to the way of nonviolence as a social strategy. When black people commit themselves to change, the method they choose to achieve the change should be chosen because they,

[25] *Ibid.*

by such choice, seek to find a new life. In the words of Frantz Fanon in *The Wretched of the Earth,* they want to "set afoot a new man."[26] However, the way to social change becomes much more urgent to the person who becomes increasingly aware of the violence of the status quo conditions which are damaging, even murderous, to very many who must live within them. Who could be at ease while some current conditions exist? But what one does is important because, as Fanon puts it: "We are forever pursued by our actions."[27] Whenever one acts, he has to ask the deeper question which all should ask, Can we move forward, and at the same time, escape becoming dizzy? Is it possible to move even in the direction of a more desirable social order without our actions pursuing us?

Carl Oglesby, in *Containment and Change,* quotes without full reference a Brazilian guerrilla as contending:

> We are in dead earnest. At stake is the humanity of man. How can ordinary men be at once warm enough to want what revolutionaries say they want (humanity), cold enough to do without remorse what they are capable of doing (cutting throats), and poised enough in the turbulence of their lives to keep the aspiration and the act both integrated and distinct. How is it that one of these passions does not invade and devour the other?[28]

Oglesby seems to conclude that the guerrilla is: "an irresponsible man whose irresponsibility has been decreed by others"; thus, he is hopeless in his commitment to a way of life that cannot spare humanity, not even the humanity of the victors.

As one reads Fanon he is surprised that he is so broadly accepted by those who adhere to the violent way, while he

---

[26] Fanon, *The Wretched of the Earth,* p. 255.

[27] *Ibid.*

[28] Richard Shaull and Carl Oglesby, *Containment and Change* (New York: Crowell, Collier, Macmillan, 1967), as quoted in Barbara Denning, "On Revolution and Equilibrium," *The War Within: Violence or Nonviolence in the Black Revolution* (New York: Sheed and Ward, 1971), p. 153.

consistently reminds us that murder cannot possibly bring to birth his new man. Surely those who know America would agree that violence and murder have kept America from achieving the full maturity of her dream, and surely such inhuman actions of violence have kept her from setting forth a new man.

The central objection to the use of nonviolence as a method or as a strategy for social change is its inability to achieve enough social change. The basic assumption is that violence does and has always without exceptions achieved a greater degree of social change. At times, such an assumption concludes that all change is positive and good and that change is always in the best interest of the people for whom it was meant. All change is not good and ethical.

Indeed, it is important that any social strategy adopted by any person or people should take serious note of what the chosen course of action does to the person or to the people in the process. Often those who embrace ways of social change do not take into account what the end results may be. The basic principle of nonviolence is its nonviolent way of insisting on one's just rights without violating the rights of anyone else. The whole strength of nonviolent action depends upon this absolute respect for the rights of the unjust oppressor, including his legal and moral rights as a person. It is only by insisting on this absolute ethical principle that the personhood of the adherent to the nonviolent way is preserved. In this way, nonviolent actions work not only for the good of those who are unjustly oppressed, but also for the good of the oppressor. Too few people want to concede that one's own well-being is always related to the other.

In this context the term nonviolence has a double meaning. On the one hand, nonviolence is a theology. On the other hand, it is a method for social action. These two meanings are integrated into the nonviolent concept because both methodology and a way of life are suggested in the social strategy for change. However, when one comes to assess the total concept of nonviolence, one

141

cannot do so without adequate and due consideration to King's thought on nonviolence as a way of life. For him, nonviolence was not a capitulation to weakness and fear; rather, nonviolence demanded that difficult kind of steadfastness which can endure indignation with dignity. For King, nonviolence always attempted to reconcile and establish a relationship rather than to humiliate the opponent. For him nonviolence was always directed against the evil rather than against the person responsible for the evil. Without exceptions, nonviolence calls the oppressed to a role of suffering rather than to a role of retaliation—while contending that the role of enduring unearned suffering is redemptive. Nonviolence is not an external attitude; it resides in the heart of the person. It is in being at peace with self that a person becomes peaceful; it is so because not being in conflict with others is the one way a person can avoid doing internal violence to his own spirit. Here conflict is not used to mean that one is *not* opposed to the other who is evil. It means that one wishes him no harm.

Machiavelli put it thus: "A man who wishes to make a profession of goodness in everything must necessarily come to grief among other men who are not good. . . . Throughout all of history, those who have most deeply touched the hearts of hardened men have been those persons who have chosen not to defend themselves with violence."

Those who reject the nonviolent way do so because they contend that those who resort to power need to be violent. If people contend that there is power only in violence, nonviolent action is probably the only means by which people can be forced to consult their conscience. Nonviolent action does not have to beg others to be nice. It can bring them to a point where being nice is recognized as the most desirable thing to do. Nonviolence places upon the enemy the pressure of one's defiance of him and the pressure of the nonviolent one's respect for his life. It always seeks to raise the level of consciousness for those engaged on both sides of struggle. The human rights of the adversary are respected, and even though his actions and his official policies are not in the best interest of the oppressed, those unjust actions, those oppressive policies become the object and focus of attention as their true natures are revealed and uncovered.

## The Nonviolent Battle

### A. The Number of Casualties

It is strange that those who choose the way of violence never assume that there will not be a large number of casualties. However, when those same people attempt to assess the effectiveness of the nonviolent way, the common view is that it is a suicidal struggle. They always cite the danger to which nonviolent action exposes life. Actually, even though in any normal violent struggle there are expected casualties, if there is any single loss of life in a nonviolent struggle there is almost always the mistaken conclusion that something is wrong. The truth of the matter is that in any struggle, whether violent or nonviolent, there will be possible loss of life; casualties are to be expected whenever one confronts the enemy as the oppressor. Even those who are adherents of nonviolence tend to feel wrongly that if they are not hurting anybody, they should not get hurt or killed themselves. One cannot forget that battles of any kind provoke a violent response because those who have power are not going to give it up voluntarily. However, few people who are critical of the casualties among the nonviolent are willing to admit that violent battle in the long run provokes more violent responses and brings greater loss of life in the ranks of the violent.

It requires insight to realize that when men have committed themselves to the nonviolent way, they have committed themselves to a higher discipline and to a more radical self-control. Those who have chosen nonviolence surely have thought through their actions. They have always, without exception, taken a longer-range view of the results, and one may be sure that they are more objective in setting their goals beyond the struggle.

## B. The Effectiveness of Nonviolence

The greater genius of the nonviolent movement is to be found in what it does both to the oppressed and to the oppressor. First of all, it is directed at the heart of the adversary, but, above all, nonviolent actions prevent the enemy from acting out of fear for his own personal security. No violence can be justified. If the enemy is unjustifiably harsh in his counteractions and if he continues to be so, he will lose the moral support which he needs to sustain his prior position. Nonviolent tactics call into the tactics the support of other nonviolent persons who are not naturally inclined to act for the cause for which the nonviolent people struggle.

As Fanon has so often reminded us, violence makes men dizzy; it disturbs the minds and the visions of the good as well as the bad; it makes for fear, insecurity, and the loss of a sense of direction and place. On the other hand, nonviolence makes men sound of mind; it gives them a sense of direction, and ethically it keeps them from mere blind mistrust of the oppressor. At least it keeps one from the point of concluding that the adversary is less than human.

## C. On Knowing the Enemy

To know the enemy is not always a mere educational task, and it is more than just acquiring a knowledge of who he is. It is, rather, also necessary to know the relative position of the enemy in order to assess what power is needed to affect those who are labeled the enemy. It is important to know their capacity to do harm; it is also important to know the ways and means by which one can negate the harm that the enemy might do. Indeed, it might do one well not to label all oppressors or masters the only enemies. Those who engage in nonviolent battle would do well to act on this simple assumption to the boldest degree. The participants in the nonviolent struggle will take note and understand that some persons, more than others, will see it as in their best interest

144

to try to destroy all opposition and will persist in attempting to do so; but the nonviolent must know the enemy to the point of knowing that others will not. One must be able to separate them and set at liberty those who would wish to be free and offer liberty to even those of a hard heart.

There are many black people who would contend that it is absurd to claim that we can avoid personal injury to the oppressor in any kind of serious struggle for social change. They would contend that men, caught up in such a struggle, are reduced to functional elements; to threaten to deprive them of their accustomed places of advantage in society is, at the same time, to threaten their very ontological being. Those who adhere to nonviolence can never see the other as a mere functional element, as a mere nothing; the other is always viewed as a person and treated as such. This is a part of the ethics of the nonviolent way of life.

## D. The Weight of Personhood

If nonviolent action is boldly taken, it asserts a higher manhood than can be overlooked by the oppressor, for it speaks to the oppressor out of the deepest of feelings; and if it is boldly taken, it always gives the acting one the conviction that he is standing up to the other like a man. Rather than expressing deep hatred by acts of revenge, nonviolence calls the actors to a higher action of the truth, and it leaves no doubt concerning one's determination to change the current state of things. In the very nonviolent process, one's hatred of the other can be forgotten because it is beside the point; the point is to change one's state of being. The point is not to give expression to the emotions that have been destroying one; the point is, rather, to so act that one can master all internal and external opposition. This is surely what Fanon means by asserting one's manhood, and it is akin to Tillich's concept of the courage to be.

One of the sure roles of the nonviolent is in demanding human behavior from others. To repeat Fanon, the nonviolent actor

145

contends: "I will impose my whole weight as a man on the other's life and show him that I am not that which he would persist in imagining. . . . What is needed is to hold oneself, like a silver, to the heart of the world, to interrupt, if necessary . . . the chain of command . . . to stand up to the world. . . . Man is human only to the extent to which he tries to impose his existence on another man in order to be recognized by him." He immediately adds: "If I close the circuit, if I prevent the accomplishment of movement in two directions, I keep the other within himself." Fanon further writes, "I do battle for the creation of a human world—that is, a world of reciprocal recognition."[29] The battle for this world, if it is to be a world wherein many persons keep their humanity, must be a battle waged nonviolently. For this is the only way men have ever been able to keep their humanity, or to keep from "becoming dizzy," as Fanon has stated it.

Indeed, many people embraced the black power movement; others merely joined the cry with swiftness. They did so, one would suspect, largely because too many of the nonviolent actions taken to that point in the civil rights movement were merely acts of petition; there was a deeply felt need among most black people for bolder action, for more radical action, and for more forthright self-assertion. The time had come for the nonviolent movement to reassess many of the old ways and to petition approaches to nonviolent assertion. Nonviolent action was, at that time, much too submissive. As Stokley Carmichael expressed it, the nonviolent movement was saying: "Look, Mr. White Man, we are only going to do what we are supposed to do; we may be on the streets, but see, we're still your good niggers, won't you help us? Look, we are your loving servants, we still love you, respect you, more than we love and respect our own lives." Only nonviolent actions, bold and daring enough, could have broken out of that conservative mind-set. The fear that he would have led nonviolence beyond that state of mentality was what finally moved many

[29] Fanon, *Black Skins, White Masks,* pp. 216, 218, 231.

persons against Dr. Martin Luther King, Jr. There is no doubt that Dr. King was moving in the direction of a more radical type of nonviolence. Such a type of nonviolent approach is more surely to be feared than violence. Indeed, it may be that this is why they pressed Dr. King to the point where he had to state and restate, again and again, the ultimate motives or goals of all of his actions. They pressured him to restate the goals precisely because oppressors feared nonviolence much more than they feared violence. What a relief the cry of black power was to the white man. He knew how to deal with violence. He has traditionally done so effectively on all sides, even to dealing ultimate death to many of the current Black Panthers. The oppressor has not yet learned how to deal with nonviolence. He still does not know how to deal with a man who has the moral initiative of love on his side.

While it was true, as Dr. Kenneth B. Clark, President of the Metropolitan Applied Research Center of City College, New York, pointed out in an address before the Southern Regional Council:

> Black Power, in spite of its ambiguity, its "no-win" premise, programmatic emptiness and its pragmatic futility, had a tremendous psychological appeal for the masses of Negroes who had . . . "nothing to lose" and some middle-class Negroes who were revolted by the empty promises and the moral dry-rot of affluent America.[30]

So the black man turned from the nonviolent way to militancy, to violence, and even to a tendency toward revolution. The act of turning and moving in a direction that was thought to be forward, the motion itself has seemingly made him dizzy. Many of the movements, which seemed to be progressive and positive, have been but meaningless and empty motion. Progress seems to be slower than ever and change, a hopeless dream.

---

[30] Benjamin Muse, *The American Negro Revolution: From Nonviolence to Black Power* (Secaucus, N. J.: Citadel Press, 1968), p. 301.

## The Current Status of the Status Quo and the Tendency Toward Revolution

### *The Status of the Status Quo*

When one reviews the current literature on the current tendency toward violence, he cannot help but conclude that the surge of all types of violence and the discovery of previously undetected forms of violence reflect a worldwide rejection of the status quo, and most types of violence are fed by a broad range of deeply felt rage and frustrations. The more disquieting thought is that too many people feel that there is no other recourse which appears feasible for achieving the necessary and desired changes at a sufficient rate. It would seem to them that power is in the hands of only the privileged, and the privileged have devised all kinds of cunning ways to abort change.

Philosophers, theologians, and poets—if they ever were inclined to accept such a prophetic task at all—have been unable to bring the reality of a present hope into the consciousness of the masses. The current upsurge of violence has achieved changes. Currently, there are those who are contending, and rightly so, that the Christian church since Constantine has traditionally accepted, benefited, and participated in the status quo. This has become so because much of the contemporary hostility that has developed toward anything associated with the establishment has brought to light the extensive degree to which Christianity has matured as a majority group. It has too wittingly become the accomplice in the development of the type of historical tradition against which such a large segment of mankind is now in open rebellion. This is even more true when one looks at the history of the black man in America and throughout the world. Indeed, it may well be that there can be no significant discussion of the New Testament in relation to problems of violence and revolution until this historical fact is seen and acknowledged as a part of the perverted Christian tradition. By repeatedly siding with law and order, the church has not only alienated itself from the oppressed, who must overthrow the status quo in order to gain equality, but it has also betrayed its inherent nonconformist vision of hope for the coming kingdom of God.

It is strange to many black people in America that the white church has regarded as heroes those Christians who participated in the resistance movement against Nazi Germany, while at the same time it has found it difficult to acknowledge those who now resist oppressive structures in our own country. This further reflects the fact that the church is allied with the status quo. It is all too true that the church has too often recovered its nonconformist tradition only when its own life was at stake. Indeed, until the church's participation in the structures of oppressive power is acknowledged and the consequences of some of the evils of that involvement are confessed, interpretations of the New Testament's teachings concerning many of the ethical problems of our time will be distorted and perverted.

## Violence and Current History

It is even more strange that much of the violence of our own time has taught us much that we should have known without such bitter experiences. It should be educationally possible for one to accept such teachings without sanctifying the violence itself; though one must grant that the blood of others has often redeemed many people from longstanding blindness. The sin of the church's involvement in the evils of our time has so often escaped us, and the fact that much of today's open violence has been a direct outgrowth of so much that the church has refused to condemn openly can no longer be ignored, even by those who are religious adherents. It is an intelligence derived from suffering, not from the rationale of any seminars. But then who else but Christians should be better equipped for such dialectical gratitude, for our tradition has regularly given thanks to God that the truth about

149

ourselves and the world has come home to us only through a violent death on a cross.

One cannot read current history without coming to the additional conclusion that the world is in a stage of transition and that the status quo is no longer a fixed period in history, if such was ever so.

It may well be that both black and white people are, as James Baldwin best puts it, "trapped in a history they do not understand." They both need an openness toward each other, if they are to "make America what America must become."[31] However, neither can rest with what is, for that which is is compelled by history to become something other than what is of the moment. In part, this means that the search for a usable future is not totally a unilateral endeavor; the ethical mandate is different, and the respective responsibilities are not the same. However, there is a theological point of focus for both. There is no turning back the clock; the status quo is no longer a fixed conception; it too has become the "not-yet" of the future. It is, as it were, a fresh entrance as that which is to come after today a projection of the future. The status quo has become the not-yet of the future, each contemporary person, mindful of the mandate of the time, must become aware of the fact that his essential existence tiptoes along the narrow ridge between the disappearing now and the ever newly-appearing not-yet. There is no status quo. The status quo is pregnant with change, and the ethos of the future is revolution.

# VIII.
# Toward an Adequate Christian Understanding of the Concept of Revolution: The Philosophical View

Revolution is increasingly becoming a recurring theme in Christian theological literature. And yet, when one sets the task for himself of giving a full and adequate assessment of much that is being espoused in support of revolution, he must confess that there seems to be too little real understanding of all that the ultimate concept of revolution would imply. Indeed, it may be that Harvey Cox is right when he contends that "we are trying to live in a period of revolution without a theology of revolution.

The development of such a theology should be the first item on the theological agenda today."[1] Because of the mood of our time, it would seem that Christian moral theology cannot, even if it would, neglect the development of some intelligible understanding of the modern concept of revolution, for the simple fact that we do live in an age of revolution and that we must relate to it in some way as Christians. This seems especially true of the black Christian. It may well be true also, as Hannah Arendt so cogently points out, that "in the contest that divides the world today and in which so much is at stake, those will probably win who understand revolution."[2]

## Toward a Clearer Definition of Revolution

The word revolution was originally an astronomical term denoting the lawfully revolving motion of the stars, which, since it was known to be beyond the influence of man and hence irresistible, was certainly characterized neither by newness nor by violence. On the contrary, the word revolution clearly indicates a recurring, cyclical movement. If used in relation to the political affairs of men on earth, it would only have been originally used to signify that the few known forms of government revolved among the peoples of the world in eternal recurrence, and with the same irresistible force which was totally external to man. Revolution, historically speaking, seemed always to render man powerless to determine any foreseeable results beyond any revolutionary actions necessary to overthrow any one form of government to achieve another.

Nothing could be farther removed from the original meaning of the word "revolution" than the idea of which all revolutionary actors have been processed and obsessed, namely, that they are agents in a process

[1] Harvey Cox, *The Secular City* (New York: Macmillan, 1965), p. 107.
[2] Arendt, *On Revolution*, p. 8.

which spells the definite end of an old order and brings about the birth of a new world.

If the case of modern revolutions were as clearcut as a textbook definition, the choice of the world "revolution" would be even more puzzling than it actually is. When the word first descended from the skies and was introduced to describe what happened on earth among mortal men, it appeared clearly as a metaphor, irresistible, ever-recurring motion to the haphazard movements, the ups and downs of human destiny. . . . In the seventeenth century, where we find the word for the first time as a political term, the metaphoric content was even closer to the original meaning of the word, for it was used for a movement of revolution back to the same pre-established point and by implication of swinging back into a pre-ordained order. Thus, the word was first used not when what we call a revolution broke out in England and Cromwell rose to the first revolutionary dictatorship, but on the contrary, in 1660, after the overthrow of the Rump Parliament and at the occasion of the restoration of the monarchy. In precisely the same sense the word was used in 1688, when the Stuarts were expelled and the kingly power was transferred to William and Mary.[3]

The word revolution, in the sense that the events through which very paradoxically the term found its definite place in political and historical usage, was not thought of as revolution at all, but rather as only a restoration of monarchical power to its former owners.

It is of interest to note the fact that the word revolution originally meant restoration—hence something which to us is its very opposite. Thus the word revolution and its meaning are not mere oddities of semantics. The revolutions of the seventeenth and eighteenth centuries, which appear to us to show all evidence of the new political spirit of the modern age, were intended to be mere political restorations.

Much more could be said of the original meaning of the word revolution, but much more important for our background discussion are the historical events which brought new meaning and content to the concept as it is used in modern times. Indeed, if we

[3] *Ibid.*, pp. 35, 36.

want to learn what a revolution is—its general implications for man as a political being, its possible political significance for the world in which we live, and its current role in modern history —we must turn to at least two of those historical events or moments when revolution made its full advent. We must turn to the point in history when revolution assumed a definite meaning and when it began to cast its spell over the minds of men, quite independent of the abuses and the cruelties and deprivations of the liberty which might well have caused people to rebel. However, in doing so, we must still recall that in even the French and the American Revolutions, somewhat representative of the historical events which did achieve something new and different politically, the leading men of both periods pleaded in all sincerity that they merely wanted to revolve back to the old times when things had been as they ought to be. They were firmly convinced that they would do no more than restore an old order of things that had been disturbed and violated by the despotism of absolute monarchy or by the abuses of colonial government. They did not seek moral ends so much as political ends. This was true in France, and it was true during the American Revolution.[4]


## The Quest for an Adequate Modern Philosophy
## of Revolution


Those who write meaningfully of current revolutions would have us note that political structures are always in need of reform, but acts of reform should be attempted with a clear view as to what ends are sought. If their views are not clear enough, it may well be noted that the greater confusion lies in the false hope which too many people place in revolutions without realizing that events and history may well attest to the fact that

[4] *Ibid.*, p. 37.

there is a demoniacal element in revolution; an outburst of desire for vehemence, of hatred and murder occur in it. In revolution, an accumulated resentment always comes into operation and vanquishes creative feelings. The sort of revolution may be desired in which there shall be no demoniacal element, but at a certain moment it always triumphs.

A revolution takes its stand beneath the flag of freedom to but a small degree; to an incomparable greater extent it stands beneath the banner of fate. . . . In revolution man desires to set himself free from slavery to the state, to an aristocracy, to the bourgeoisie, to lying sanctities and falls into slavery to a new tyranny.[5]

Nikolai Berdyaev seems to be suggesting that there are those uncontrollable elements in all revolutions which take over and sweep them on. It should be clear if such is the case that this is all the more reason that the goals of all revolutions need to be written into the ideals to be achieved beyond revolution. Indeed, history has taught us that the risk inherent in all revolutions is otherwise too great. These clear dangers come when men are pushed, as are many black men, to the point that they contend that any change is better than current conditions.

Many current revolutionary philosophers are one in their concern that there are many even greater dangers to be found in all revolutions, especially for those who are to become active participants in the revolution. We shall now turn to look objectively at some of the dangers which should be noted by those who would be participants in revolutions.

First of all, revolutionary philosophers point out that there is the danger of even good persons becoming totally consumed by the events of the revolution, so much so that one loses all sense of virtue. This danger was described in The Revolutionary Catechism as follows:

The revolutionary is a dedicated man. He has no interests, no business, no emotions, no attachments, no property, not even a name. In his

[5] Berdyaev, *Slavery and Freedom,* p. 190.

innermost depths he has broken all ties with the social order. He knows but one science, that of destruction. The tender sentiments of family, friendship, love, and gratitude must be subjugated to the single cold passion of the revolutionary cause.[6]

The above is a man who has lost his humanity in actions which have for him no meaning beyond the mere action. In her great and most insightful book, *On Revolution,* Hannah Arendt gives an extensive treatment of many of the leading personalities of past revolutions. However, she gives special attention to Robespierre, one of the principal personalities of the French Revolution. Her penetrating and thoughtful insights conclude that though Robespierre was a man of great character and clear virtue before the revolution, something radical took place inside him which changed him completely during the course of the French Revolution. Professor Arendt contends that Robespierre became so obsessed with the hunt for hypocrites that he forgot that such a search is always boundless and can produce nothing but demoralization. Arendt also contends that Robespierre thus carried the conflicts of the soul into politics, where they became murderous because they were insoluble.

Robespierre's insane lack of trust in others, even in his closest friends, sprang ultimately from his not so insane but quite normal suspicion of himself. Since his very credo forced him to play the "incorruptible" in public every day and to display his virtue, to open his heart as he understood it, at least once a week, how could he be sure that he was not the one thing he probably feared most in his life, a hypocrite? [7]

If, in Robespierre's own words, he confesses that patriotism is a thing of the heart, then the reign in time of revolution seems bound to be at worst the rule of hypocrisy, and at best a never-ending fight to ferret out the hypocrites, a fight which could only have ended in defeat because of the simple fact that it is always

[6] Quoted by Roland Gaucher, *The Terrorists, from Tsarist Russia to the O.A.S.* *(London: Secker & Warburg, 1968), p. 3.*

[7] *Arendt, On Revolution,* p. 92.

impossible, especially in times of national crisis, to distinguish between true and false patriots. Who can point out the hypocrite? Yet, how often do we try?

The heart of the inner man knows many such intimate personal struggles, and it also knows too well that what appeared straight when hidden may well also appear crooked when it is displayed.

The revolutionary always has to come to that point when he has to deal with others. It is many times at this point that his own personal motives remain dark; they do not shine but are hidden not only from others but most of the time from himself. Hence, the search for motives, the ever current demand that everybody display in public, is his innermost motivation as a revolutionary. It actually demands the impossible and all to often transforms the participants into hypocrites. Indeed, the moment the demand for the display of motives begins, hypocrisy begins to poison all human relations.

Secondly, revolutionary philosophers contend further that external forces, both personal and impersonal, may take over the direction and the events of the revolution, so that they are no longer controllable.

In one of his more reflective moments, late in the French Revolution, Robespierre seems to suggest that the revolution got out of hand because some external force took over. But the Revolution unmasked its children before proceeding to devour them one by one; it was the war upon hypocrisy that transformed Robespierre's dictatorship into a Reign of Terror, and the outstanding characteristic of this period was the self-purging of the rulers.[8]

Thirdly, if we take seriously Arendt's and Berdyaev's suggestions and if we accept the views of many other revolutionary philosophers that there are also external factors which tend to take over revolutions, then we must come to a third warning concerning revolution. It is that there is always a danger of the loss of the

[8] *Ibid.*, p. 94.

ideal and a clear sense of the humane moral principle of the revolutionary struggle. The humane moral principle is always blurred whenever the revolutionary comes to the point where he must judge another's motives. It always follows that when the central purpose of the revolution has gone, those who participate are always in trouble because that which is seemingly external is sure to take hold.

Jurgen Moltmann contends that under certain conditions the use of revolutionary violence can be justified by humane goals. However, he is not too sure that such justification can be assured, and so he concludes that unless it is possible and assured, "revolutionary violence cannot be made meaningful or appropriate. Unless every possible means is put to use, the revolutionary future is not worth committing one's self to."[9] One wonders if any black person can embrace Moltmann's position when he advises that "people must be able to combine what they desire with what is objectively possible and what they can subjectively accomplish."[10] Such a statement is hard for an oppressed person to accept within the current time.

Indeed, if a revolution can be this rational and if the aims can be reconceived, then one wonders if some more rational approach cannot be found. It would seem that Moltmann is nearer right when he reminds us:

> If the revolutionary goal is a more fully realized humanity, then revolutionaries cannot afford to be inhuman during the so-called transitional period. Already, on the way, we must directly begin with the future and make life truly human during the transitional period. . . . It follows, therefore, that a revolution of the present for the benefit of a better and more humane future must not mold itself after the strategies of the world to be overthrown. Only with great restraint can revolutionaries enter the diabolical circle of violence and counterviolence if they are ever to conquer and abolish it as a whole. . . . How

[9] Moltmann, *Religion, Revolution and The Future,* p. 143.
[10] *Ibid.*

are we to bring about the kingdom of nonviolent brotherhood with the help of violent action?[11]

These words of Moltmann cannot be read without recalling the teachings of Martin Luther King, Jr., for it was he who thought and acted out a deep dimension of truth, which was not dependent on political power and the rules of its games. In a very real sense, the true revolutionary must not allow the law of the opposition or the oppressor to prescribe his own course of action or response; if he does, he cannot become a part of the new humanity. Any means may be appropriate, but they must be different and better than those of the oppressor if they would bewilder the opposition.[12]

Finally, within this context, it is clear that a mere pointing out of the dangers of revolution must not be equated with an antirevolutionary attitude, nor an absolute conclusion against revolution. Surely no oppressed person can fully conclude with Hannah Arendt when she contends that

> freedom has been better preserved in countries where no revolution ever broke out, no matter how outrageous the circumstances of the powers that be, and there exists more civil liberties even in countries where the revolution was defeated than in those where revolutions have been victorious.[13]

One may well not agree in such a conclusion; however, it must be open to great question.

However, in quite another context, Arendt asserts with more truth that "revolutionaries tend to establish the same type of government which they overthrow."[14] If such is true, then, the much deeper concern may well be the question of whether or not liberation and freedom can be established by mere means of

[11] *Ibid.*

[12] For a larger discussion of revolution in a more theological context, see chapter 7 of Major J. Jones' book *Black Awareness: A Theology of Hope*, pp. 87 ff.

[13] Arendt, *On Revolution*, p. 111.

[14] *Ibid.*, p. 154.

revolution? If one assumes such to be possible, then the criterion for action is the measure of the possible transformation. Skill is needed to bring together the opponents, the means, and the end in such a creative tension that the hoped-for effect will or can be achieved. It is to this end that all revolutionaries must address themselves before the act. The person who chooses to become a part of a revolution must never forget the ever present risk, and he must be willing to assess the full meaning of revolution and its implications for the individual.

## Jesus Christ and the Tendency Toward Revolution

In the current tendency toward revolution, especially when there are attempts to make it Christian and to interpret Jesus as revolutionary, a Christian must take care that there is no misreading of the New Testament. There are many current Christians who tend to misinterpret the New Testament in an attempt to make Jesus fit their preconceived idea that he was a zealot or a violent one. They do so with no regard for the fact that Jesus was free of specific ideologies. In all of the current discussions regarding the relationship of Jesus to the phenomenon of revolution, the key factor is Jesus' own attitude toward the situations and the movements of his time. Jesus was so close to God, his expectations of the kingdom of God were so real, his faith was so sure that within this kingdom justice would prevail, that one would question if his concept of the kingdom would include any narrow interests. His deep faith in God's rule would cause his thoughts to transcend the framework of those groups which supported the narrow political orders in Palestine as well as of those who opposed it with a counterforce.[15] It is in this light that Cullmann contends that Jesus was no narrowminded person of special personal political interests.

[15] Oscar Cullmann, *Jesus and the Revolutionaries* (New York: Harper & Row, 1970), pp. vii, viii.

The effort to make Jesus a revolutionary is very old, having begun in the eighteenth century by H. S. Reumarus. His "On the Intentions of Jesus" is now available in the *Lives of Jesus* series published by Fortress Press and edited by L. E. Keck. In S. G. F. Brandon's *Jesus and the Zealots,* he has cogently argued that Jesus and his followers within the early church as well were zealots.[16]

However, Oscar Cullman takes the added position that "Jesus in his proclamation most sharply condemned the social injustice of his time. Also here he shared an essential concern of the zealots. He judged this entire problem in the light of the Kingdom of God."[17]

By rooting Jesus in a kind of eschatological radicalism, Cullmann's contention is that he could not have been a thoroughgoing Zealot in any sense of the word. He is a liberator, but his liberation is spiritual. Yet, having thus concluded, Cullmann does not take the position that Jesus was not concerned with the current issues of his time, neither does he take the position that he would not be concerned with the contemporary political issues of his time. Cullmann rightly concludes that

> Christians, who today share responsibility for reforms, should freely and competently make use of the technical means which the modern world offers them, but they should not wish to declare that along with their technical proficiency they also take their ultimate norms from the world instead of from the gospel.[18]

Although Jesus was not a Zealot, he nevertheless was a revolutionary in quite a different sense, and this is the one thing that set him above the categories of his time. He is more than a Zealot, he was and is more than a mere black Messiah, he was and is the

[16] S. G. F. Brandon, *Jesus and the Zealots* (New York: Stein & Day, 1968).

[17] Cullmann, *Jesus and the Revolutionaries,* p. 24 ff.

[18] *Ibid.,* p. 57.

one that is always coming, and it is he who always calls for a complete break with the present order. Carl E. Braaten is right when he reminds us that "politics presupposes too much continuity"; indeed, the liberating changes which ought be sought are much deeper and more lasting. The powers and principalities, of which political structures and programs are but representative, need much more than the type of treatment that mere present revolutionary actions would suggest. If Braaten is right in his assessment, Jesus was not a child of the political structures of his time because present realities are never all they seem to be at any given time in history; they are but signs pointing beyond themselves. Current events have meaning only if they can be seen as they are and can also be interpreted in the light of the future. This suggestion relates the means always, in some sense, to the end and thus the future.

There is such an urgency about change until it always demands a radical conversion within the life of those who heard. To call for revolution meant to commit one's self to change. Jesus was clear in his demand that you cannot wait to change until after the revolution—You must do it now.[19]

This need for radical change has two implications for the current tendency toward revolution that should be noted in this context. First of all, if one—black or white—takes Carl Braaten's model of Jesus as a revolutionary, he is called to a radical ethical orientation that commits him to a humane principle that transcends the all current political categories. It is a category which calls one to an "unconditional surrender to absolute love—love to God and to fellowmen."[20] This makes it impossible, as both Martin Luther King and Carl Braaten would hold, to love just those on the right side or on the left side. They both would contend, with agreement, that you must not just love the beautiful

[19] Carl E. Braaten, *Christ and Counter-Christ* (Philadelphia: Fortress Press, 1972), p. 111, 112 ff.

[20] *Ibid.*

people and hate the ugly, you must not just love those who are politically palatable to you and hate those who are not. To be the kind of revolutionary Jesus was, one must affirm every man as brother—even one's enemy. "The true revolutionary prays for the one who persecutes him. It is easy and natural to curse, hate, and kill. All of that requires no revolution at all, but only to go with the adrenalin flow."[21] Secondly, at the other end of the scale is quite another type of person. He is the person lost or caught up in revolutionary action without sufficient moral foundations. And without moral foundations, the revolutionary becomes dizzy. A person "cannot bypass the concern for morality in any quest for power."[22] Power is never good unless the person who has it is good and has a clear sense of the ethical. Without moral foundations, how can many persons "go forward all the time, night and day, in the company of man, in the company of all men."[23]

But how can any ethical person go forward in the company of all men if he is willing to kill to the point of becoming less than the ethically responsible person of which Carl Oglesby so often speaks in *Containment and Change*? [24] It may be that Nikolai Berdyaev is right when he reminds us that in revolution man always desires to set himself free from something or someone. It may be slavery to the state, it may be slavery to an aristocracy, it may be slavery to the bourgeoisie, it may be slavery to lying sanctities. However, if he chooses the way of the mere political revolutionary, he falls into slavery to a new tyranny.[25] He falls into slavery to a lesser self, to a lower self that has lost its humanity. Those philosophers who write on revolution have the basic contention that there is a demoniacal element in revolution. Eventually there develops an intense unquenchable desire for vengeance, and almost without exceptions, hatred and murders

[21] See Martin Luther King's *Where Do We Go From Here: Chaos or Community?*, pp. 54-66.

[22] Fanon, *The Wretched of the Earth*, 255 ff.

[23] *Ibid.*

[24] Shaull and Oglesby, *Containment and Change*, p. 146.

[25] Berdyaev, *Slavery and Freedom*, p. 190.

prevail. Something else takes hold over which persons, individually and collectively, seem to lack the moral ability to control. It may be that this is why those moral philosophers who write on revolution further contend that in revolution one is in danger of becoming dizzy. To return to Braaten's model, the spirit exampled in Jesus breaks down the divisions which separate men by raising up those at the bottom. "The goal of this proletarian prejudice is the unity of humanity, not a division of it."[26] In such an apocalyptic concept of revolution there is irony, paradox, and esoteric logic in the new climate to be achieved. The last shall be the first, and the first shall be the last. The one who would be the leader would become the servant. The back of the hierarchical model is broken with this reversal of roles. The entire meaning of being number one is altered. As one reads more of Braaten's model of Jesus, he wonders if this role fits the prior servant or slave. Yet, one is sure this is the required role of the ex-slave as well as the ex-master.

Finally, it would seem that many who write of the future have overlooked the fact that the "now" facet of the future may well be but a flickering glimpse of what is to come. If theologians, unmindful of the implications of the revolutionary spirit, keep talking as if this were the way, then mankind will not glean from them what the moral imperative should be. They may seek salvation without suffering, and in the hours of pain, tribulation, anguish, and misery, they may come too soon to the point of despair and hopelessness. One is sure this note should be sounded in the black community. First because the servant and suffering role seems to be over before the responsible role begins. Secondly, because suffering is not the spirit of the new black man's mind-set.

Against categorizing Jesus among the Zealots or the revolutionaries, Oscar Cullmann concludes that "there are many

---

[26] Braaten, *Christ and Counter-Christ,* p. 113.

other clues that place Jesus against the political religion of the Zealots. Cullmann asserts that Jesus agreed with the Zealots' hope for the Kingdom of God, but not that it would come in the style of the Zealots."[27] "Yet, he did not flee to the wilderness or attempt a premature flight from the world. . . . . Jesus took his revolution downtown into the midst of all the realities of the world."[28] Indeed, Jesus was not a politician, but politics were linked to the eschatology that Jesus proclaimed and lived. He was absolute in his call for change; for him, the individual and society could not survive a spiritual revolution. Jesus' revolution had eschatological dimensions that called for total change, and this was why too many of the people of his time did not accept him then—and this is why so many people, black and white, cannot fully accept him now.

Carl Braaten rightly makes the clearer point that "Jesus' revolution was more than political. . . . . Politics presuppose too much continuity."[29] As has been cited above, Braaten's contention is that political revolution is only surface revolution, thus lacking the eschatological dimensions necessary for the kind of complete change to which the Jesus revolution always calls men. In quite another context, this may well be why Hannah Arendt could make the point that the American Revolution could take place under the inspiration of the beautiful words of the Declaration of Independence, that all men are created equal, and yet give no real thought to the fact that there were hundreds of slaves who were excluded.

The total change to which Jesus called men would have made such isolation and insensitivity impossible; under his rule, the man of the American Revolution could not have overlooked the plight of the poor, they could not have excluded the slave, they

[27] Cullmann, *Jesus and the Revolutionaries,* pp. 51 ff.

[28] Braaten, *Christ and Counter-Christ,* p. 106.

[29] *Ibid.,* pp. 110 ff.

could not have omitted any person from the changes achieved by the revolution. But the revolution was merely political, and it did not require the eschatological dimensions of which Braaten so cogently speaks.

In this context, it is also interesting to note that one of the most radical interpretations of Jesus is the attempt not only to make him a Zealot, but to make him black as well. Albert B. Cleage, Jr.,[30] tends to give Jesus a total reorientation toward a narrow black concern alone. He makes Jesus a black political Zealot and adopts him totally to the black cause with little concern for any other people or any other concerns. Like James H. Cone, he relates Jesus only to the black struggle for liberation. Most theologians, black and white, now attempting to develop a theology of revolution would tend to relate Jesus to the black struggle, and most writers would make the black cause but one of his concerns as a current revolutionary.

One can only conclude that these New Testament interpretations giving undue support to violence and revolution represent at best: (1) the ideological misuse of the New Testament; (2) a misunderstanding of Jesus' own freedom from ideology, narrow concerns; and (3) a message from God that is too small to transcend the now of the moment. Jesus was and still is a man for all seasons and a liberator adequate for all persons living in our times.

Living, as it were, in a world so engrossed in revolution, the black Christian cannot avoid giving it some serious assessment. Indeed, so much is at stake until he must be a part of those who understand revolution. There must be full understanding of the concept, not with the intent to win a political revolution as such, but because if it takes place in spite of him, he must be ready to accept some responsibility for the outcome and the future. The objectives are too high, the scale of justice, the quality of liberation, the kind of freedom to be established, and ultimately the

[30] Albert B. Cleage, *The Black Messiah* (New York: Sheed & Ward, 1968).

shape of society are at stake. With the above objective look at revolution from the more general standpoint of philosophy now, some more related and restricted views of Christian ethics are needed within this context to understand the fuller ethical problems which revolution poses for the Christian.

# IX.
# Ethical Issues in the Development of a Theology of Revolution

## Basic Ethical Issues

In the increasing number of current theologians and philosophers that are now calling for a fuller understanding of revolution, and in the many published books which extend some degree of ethical and theological justifications for revolutions, one finds himself with many lingering questions as to whether there can be an authentic Christian, ethical, or theological justification for revolution.

This book takes the position that taken in its fullest ethical and political connotations, revolution cannot be justified by Christian ethics or theology; if when we speak of revolution, we mean all that is implied in its fullest possible political implications. However, this is not to say that Christian theology and ethics should not come to grips with revolution as a political concept and as an ideological movement of our time. Though it may be the position of this book that there are deep moral problems in any attempt to develop an authentic theological or ethical justification for revolution, it does not follow that there is the implied view that there should not be a full theological or ethical assessment of the concept of revolution in order to give the Christian some objective theological and ethical guidelines to inform his moral judgment while he is living in a world of revolution. Especially is this true of the black Christian. Any attempt to develop a theology of revolution is ethically problematic for the following reasons, which no rational Christian can overlook.

First, no matter how a Christian may relate to a revolution, he must never be under the mistaken illusion that he can, as a participant, control all of the ultimate or possible events of revolutionary actions. The Christian must not be misled in the belief that revolutionary actions in the modern world might not mean possible violence, and that violence may not mean possible killing, and that he will not have to become a part of such ultimate actions.

Secondly, if the Christian comes to grips with the ultimate ethical implications of the sanctity of life, he must come to grips with his moral obligation which requires that he give careful attention to what the gift of life means from both religious and nonreligious frames of reference. Such attention must include all human life; there can be no exceptions.

Thirdly, it would seem, that the Christian man has no other alternative but to grope for the middle ground on which evil can be successfully resisted and violence and ultimate killing can be avoided. If such is not possible, then the Christian has no other course open but to resist evil in whatever manner he deems

169

appropriate, knowing the ethical implications of his actions. The black Christian faces the added problem of evils which threaten his own ontological being where there is no middle ground. His moral obligations under such conditions are all the more urgent. The above introduction brings us to the heart of the matter—how important is human life?

## The Sanctity of Life Dilemma

An experiential understanding of the sanctity of life concept can best be called to our attention in this context by cogent arguments put forth by Edward Shils and P. D. Medawar justifying the fuller concept of the sanctity of life. Pointing to what seems to be an almost instinctive human revulsion at any and every form of contrived intervention in human life, Shils believes such revulsions are not merely related to the belief that man is a creature of God. On the contrary, he contends that the Christian belief in the sanctity of life has been greatly augmented and sustained by a much "deeper proto-religious 'natural metaphysic,' which also accounts for the respect given human life by those who are neither Christian nor religious."[1]

Shils states:

> The chief feature of the proto-religious "natural metaphysic" is the affirmation that life is sacred. It is believed to be sacred not because it is a manifestation of a transcendent creator from whom life comes; it is believed to be sacred because it is life. . . . . The idea of sacredness is generated by the primordial experience of being alive, of experiencing the elemental sensation of vitality and the elemental fear of its extension. . . . If life were not viewed as sacred, then nothing else would be sacred. . . . The question still remains: Is human life really sacred? I answer that it is, self-evidently. Its sacredness is the most primordial of experience.[2]

[1] Edward Shils, "The Sanctity of Life" *Life or Death: Ethics and Options* (Seattle, Wash.: University of Washington Press, 1968), p. 9.

[2] *Ibid.*, pp. 12, 14, 18.

There is, of course, still room for some persons to contend that life is not made sacred by either the religious or the nonreligious criteria. They would assign life a lesser value, deriving its worth from other nonmoral criteria derived from the social context. This is how many whites still view all black people. Others would hold that an appeal to either is not a valid reason to reject a needed revolutionary commitment on the basis of the possibility that killing might be required, and that one would be a part of it.

It is true that those who take either of the above positions affirming the sacredness of human life from either a religious or nonreligious frame of reference will be accused by others, who may not adhere to such a view, as being hung up on human life. However, this should be true for every ethically rational human being, black or white, religious or nonreligious. Indeed, it may well be that every Christian who accepts Jesus Christ as his example will have to deal with the ultimate question as to whether he takes the principle of the sanctity of life so seriously that he would rather give his own life than take the life of another, even when the other is the aggressor. This was the dilemma that Jesus faced on the cross. He regarded life so highly that he chose rather to give up his own life.

## Deeper Theological and Ethical Problems with Revolution

Surely the revolutionary would not agree with Paul Ramsey's theological view: ''A man's dignity is an overflow from God's dealing with him, and not primarily an anticipation of anything he will ever be by himself alone. The value of a human life is ultimately grounded in the value God is placing on it.''[3]

Ramsey makes two points very clear in this context. First, he reminds us that in the religious view the sanctity of human life is

[3] Paul Ramsey, "The Morality of Abortion," *Life or Death: Ethics and Options*, p. 71.

not a function of the worth any human being might attribute to it; this, therefore, precludes a discussion of any degree of relative worth a human being may have or may acquire.

Secondly, Ramsey contends that a man's life "is entirely an ordination, a loan, and a stewardship. His essence is his existence before God and to God, and it is from him. . . . . It is because God has said 'yes' to life, man's 'yes' should echo his."[4]

If one takes Edward Shils or Paul Ramsey seriously, then it would be impossible to develop a Christian theology which would seek to extend ethical or theological justifications for the negation or violation of the sanctity of life, even for a high and noble cause. However, even if the cause did justify a revolution and the price in the loss of human life were high, how would we escape the grave tragedy described by Richard Barnet in *Intervention and Revolution*? Speaking of the revolutionary, Barnet contends that "the revolutionary, even when he is fired by a righteous cause, often marks his success by reverting to the political type which he supplants. He becomes a political intriguer, a persecutor of his critics, a lover of luxury, or an addict of personal adultation."[5] One might also recall within this context that in Karl Barth's theology of creation, he emphasizes the respect due human life. In such an emphasis, Barth gives the word respect a deep connotation, indicating that we should stand in awe of that human life which God has granted man.

> Respect is man's astonishment, humility, and awe at a fact in which he meets something of superior majesty, dignity, holiness, a mystery which compels him to withdraw and keep his distance, to handle it modestly, circumspectly, and carefully. . . . In human life, he meets something superior.[6]

Helmut Thielicke also stresses that

[4] *Ibid.*, pp. 72, 73, 76.

[5] For a larger view of this concept, see Richard Barnet's *Intervention and Revolution* (New York: New American Library, 1972).

[6] Karl Barth, *Church Dogmatics* (Edinburgh, Scotland: T. and T. Clark, 1961), p. 355.

a theory of "alien dignity" protects human life from being subjected to utilitarian treatment at the hands of other human beings, the measure of human value is not man's "functional proficiency" or "pragmatic utility," but rather "the sacrificial love which God has invested in him."[7]

Martin J. Buss further contends that "theologically . . . the worth of man lies in his being addressed by a diety."[8]

If, theologically, man is called to a high respect for the sanctity of life, then it follows that ethically it would be hard to develop a moral justification for willing the death of another human being. However, before we turn to the more ethical problem, let us turn to the rational ethical view.

## The Rational Ethical Problem with Revolution

It must be noted that even if there were no deeper theological problems with revolution, there still would be a mere rational ethical problem. If one takes seriously Immanuel Kant's formulation of the moral imperative, he must contend that we are all under a moral obligation to "act in such a way that we will always treat humanity, whether in our own person or in the person of another, never simply as a means, but always at the same time as an end."[9] If the Christian man, be he white or black, attributes any value to life at all, the categorical imperative of duty, which is ultimately derived from God, brings him face to face with the fact that he cannot assign supreme value to life, except where he also accepts, to some degree, the stewardship and the belief in the sanctity of life. This is the supreme value of life and thus is more in keeping with Christian theological constructs.

[7] Helmut Thielicke, *The Ethics of Sex* (New York: Harper & Row, 1934), p. 231.

[8] Martin J. Buss, "The Beginning of Life as an Ethical Principle," *The Journal of Religion* (July, 1967), p. 249.

[9] Immanuel Kant, *Fundamental Principles of the Metaphysic of Morals*. See translation by T. K. Abbott (Longmans, Green, 1873).

Indeed, if one accepts the fact that life has supreme value, and that it is ordained by God, then he must come to grips with the ultimate question as to whether he can support, justify, or participate in any actions which ignore or violate life as a trust. One must have respect for the lives of others because God is the Lord of all life and death. No black or white Christian can view life as less than a trust. This is but one way of proclaiming that man holds his own life in trust and yet another way of saying that no man can take it upon himself to place himself as total master over the life of another. To confess that God is Lord of all life and death can be no less than to affirm that man is a creature, owing his existence, his value, and his ultimate destiny to God. Granted that this view of life is not an absolute principle with no exceptions, it is still a general guide which cannot be too greatly ignored within any particular context or situation.

## Toward an Ethic of Distress

Such a context would not be complete unless the Christian frankly stated that there might well be occasions when under certain crisis conditions the Christian might find it impossible to stand aside and let evil have its way. Often the Christian has no ethical choice; he must either take sides and fight for an evil and oppressive regime, or he must take sides with what he feels to be a potentially better political or social order. There are times when there is no other choice. Indeed, when a Christian feels that he must enter the arena of revolutionary action, that he has no other choice, he must always cope with the possibility that there may be a breakdown of order or of politics and the ultimate possibility that violence will occur. He must also face the fact that killing may ensue, and that he will be a part of the ultimate outcome.

Under such conditions, first of all, it would seem that there can be no theology of revolution which does not come to grips, in some way, with the question of whether it is at all possible to extend a theological or Christian ethical justification for one human being killing another human being.[10] Is killing ever right?

Secondly, the Christian theologican who attempts to construct a theology of revolution must face the ultimate risk of whether violent means can ever produce enough good to justify the ends. Without exception, any theology of revolution has to face the question of whether it could ever support, theologically or ethically, the act of a Christian killing even the neighbor or the enemy whom he is obligated as a Christian to love.

Whether the call for revolution be a first or a last resort, the question the Christian faces in relation to violence is whether he can kill another person. Does killing ever become for the Christian ethically right on any occasion, in any war, even in a just war? Whether the killing is intentional or unintentional, the problem is the same for the Christian. Even in contextual or situational ethics, if one is committed under God to love the neighbor, does it not seem impossible to reconcile the act of killing the neighbor that one is ethically committed under God to love? Is it at all possible for one to give adherence to the concept of the sacredness of persons or to the sanctity of life concept and at the same time will the destruction of life? It would seem that it is impossible for the Christian to answer such questions in the affirmative.

Within this context, there has been no attempt to deal with extreme conditions that may make revolution and the possible killing of a human being necessary. It is to contend that, rather than attempting to justify such extreme actions or possible killing theologically, it would seem that the Christian should recognize revolution or the act of killing for what they are. The act of killing is, indeed, a violent moment. It is an unchristian and unethical moment. Paul Ricoeur in his *History and Truth* has cogently described the violent moment as a time when there is need for an ethic of distress; it is a time when the Christian recognizes that

---

[10] Such a view to killing is explained in some lesser degree in another context in Major J. Jones, *Black Awareness: A Theology of Hope,* pp. 87 ff.

175

his action in general or the violent moment in particular can no longer be called Christian, that there can be no possible theological or ethical justification. Ricoeur is right in contending that an ethic of distress is preferable to an ethic which anticipates the legitimacy of either killing or the ethic of pure passivism, which adopts the victim role. Thus, Ricoeur further concludes that the ethic of distress seems to be a better alternative for a Christian than a theology of revolution, which sets out in advance to justify all the principles of the violent moment or revolution.[11] Indeed, the time often comes when the Christian feels that he cannot remain neutral. This is the moment when it would be more honest and moral for the Christian to adopt an ethic of distress admitting to himself and to his God that his future actions beyond this point are not Christian or ethical. In adopting an ethic of distress, the Christian seeks no ethical justification for what he feels he must do within the context of the movement, because he knows that there can be no such justification for what he is about. Such a stance would, it seems, prevent all impossible attempts to construct a blanket theological justification for so much that is wrong with revolution, war, the killing of other human beings.

Thirdly, even if the Christian could conceivably answer in the affirmative that it is possible to justify killing another person whom he is obligated to love, there would still be the much deeper ethical question of the possible personal cost and the personal sacrifice of his own total humanity during a time of revolution or in the act of killing, a price that is ultimately required of all revolutionaries.

> The revolutionary must be prepared, for the sake of the revolution, to exploit friendships, betray personal trust, to tell lies. Especially in guerrilla warfare, the revolutionary should be ready to utilize torture, the most degrading and dehumanizing violation of humanity. In short, the revolutionary is prepared to act in specifics against all his most

[11] Paul Ricoeur, *History and Truth* (Evanston, Ill.: Northwestern University Press, 1965), pp. 243, 244.

human and compassionate instincts in order to achieve the highest good of the revolutionary purpose. The more the revolutionary is impulsed by the hard necessities of revolution, the more essential it becomes for him to think through the humanizing rationale, the justification, of the revolution. . . .

If the revolution is achieved at the price of his own humanity, the revolutionary becomes the most pathetic of figures. He may claim that he is prepared to sacrifice his own humanity for the sake of a new and more just humanizing order, but the man who has lost his own humanity cannot bestow the gift of humanity on others.[12]

Fourth, a theological justification for revolution is problematic because the revolutionary, at some point ceases to be his own person. He is either a person directed by other persons or external historical events. He does, in fact, become a rebel. But the more frightening thing about a rebel is that too often he is no longer a responsible person in charge of his own destiny.

Carl Oglesby and Richard Shaull in *Containment and Change* contend that "the rebel is an irresponsible man whose irresponsibility has been decreed by others. . . . . His motivating vision of change is, at root, a vision of something absent."[13]

While one cannot possibly accept Oglesby's full conclusion, his contentions are sufficient to indicate that to choose the way of revolution is to take a grave risk; it is as if one takes a plunge into an abyss from which there may not be a sure return.

It would seem that one can ill afford the risk of what might be suggested by Colin Morris.

The Christian who becomes revolutionary takes the risk that in a world locked up in the past, the blow which opens the way to the future may count as the "one thing needful" about which Jesus talked. He steps beyond any traditional understanding of Jesus into a spiritual and ethical No Man's Land in the hope that the future is where God is.[14]

---

[12] Peter Berger and Richard J. Neubus, *Movement and Revolution: On American Radicalism* (New York: Doubleday, 1970), pp. 158, 159.

[13] Oglesby and Shaull, *Containment and Change,* p. 146.

[14] Morris, *Unyoung, Uncolored, Unpoor,* p. 157.

Such is noble talk, but as one looks at what is taking place among those who live with the current revolutionary zeal, he wonders if, indeed, their religion can sustain them against the ever present dangers of becoming less than human?

Indeed, if violent revolution can be less than rational, and if its aims cannot be preconceived, then one wonders if some other option cannot be found to perfect social and political change. The true revolutionary must not allow the law of the opposition to prescribe his own course of action or response within any context—otherwise he cannot become a part of the new future humanity. Any means may well be appropriate, but they must be different and better means than those of the opposition, if they would bewilder the opposition.

Finally, it must be clear that a mere pointing out of the dangers of revolution must not be equated with an antirevolutionary attitude or with an absolute conclusion against revolutionary change; it rather calls for a fixing on new ways to revolutionarily achieve change. Indeed, can we do other than agree with Dr. Martin Luther King, Jr., after looking at many historic accounts of revolution?

> The ultimate weakness of violence is that it is a descending spiral, begetting the very thing it seeks to destroy. Instead of diminishing evil, it multiplies it. Through violence, you may murder the liar, but you cannot murder the lie, nor establish the truth. Through violence, you may murder the hater, but you do not murder hate. So it goes. Returning violence for violence multiplies violence, adding deeper darkness to a night already devoid of stars. Darkness cannot drive out darkness; only light can do that. Hate cannot drive out hate, only love can do that.[15]

The search for a usable future must be an effective search; it must not be, it cannot be, a fruitless pursuit. It must be a rational way that assures all who walk therein a victory that is complete and void of dizziness.

[15] King, *Where Do We Go From Here: Chaos or Community?* pp. 54-66.

# X.
# The Now and the Not Yet Formulations for an Ethic of Hope

Christian realism may well lead one to the conclusion that we live in a world of conflict, that violence is natural and moral for man and society. If this realism scandalizes the Christian, it is because he makes the mistake of thinking that what is natural or normal is good and what is necessary is legitimate. To achieve true freedom one has to escape necessity; to achieve freedom is, rather, to live above what seems to be the necessary. Man becomes free through his choice of a higher way than the mere ordinary or the way of violence and necessity.

In a real sense, then, the black man of the future must be a man

179

who lives above the level of the natural, the normal, or even the necessary. He must be one who accepts only that which is for him an ultimate way into the future. Men of little minds cannot lead, for there may not be enough visible signs to guide little minds into a future void of dreams. That which will guide the mind of the black man of the future are the goals of his desire. Hope, in any sense of the word, depends upon such desires being raised so high that he will lift himself upward to a level above the ordinary in achieving them. Black people of the future cannot be driven, they cannot be coerced, they can only be led by the drawing powers of their own desires. Black people of America will be free only when they make up their minds that they are free and start to act like they are free. With this action, it can become a reality.

Hope is central to the desires which call black people into the future, and such a hope cannot be disappointed. Hope in all ages has remained hope against all temptations of nihilism; for life is always both inclusive and tentative. Hope has not been victorious anywhere, but neither has hope ever been frustrated anywhere. It is hope's true nature not to be fully realized, and yet it is also hope's true nature not to be frustrated or fully defeated. However, hope must always have a kind of realism about it, and a part of that realism must include the knowledge that among black people there can be no human dignity if want is not ended nor human happiness until the law is just and ethical. There can be no happiness or dignity until men can live with their heads held high But for such to be so, black people must make it so by their attitude concerning what is just. Too many black people talk about a revolution void of hope. A man makes revolution because he has no other options; a boy makes revolution because he has no other thoughts. If revolution is the goal of black people, nothing other than revolution will do. If a changed and a just society are the goals, there may be several ways to achieve such changes. However, if one is honest, it must be admitted that there are those who have come to the point of thinking revolution because they see no other reasonable way to achieve needed reforms. They do not see that successfully achieved political and social reforms can have revolutionary consequences. It must be pointed out further that those who have arrived at the current point of thinking revolution have come by different routes. Some have come out of the great tribulations of years of honest struggle for reform, while others have come out of the way of theoretical consideration in which it has become obvious that the goals they seek cannot be achieved within the framework of the prevailing economic, social, or political order.

In seeking the future, black people are confronted with the critical need to make a decision as to who will lead them into the future, and they should decide what kind of future they are going to seek. It may well be time to ask: "Who speaks for black people?" Yet, in too many cases, the voices of those who call black people into the future are voices that are unclear about the ethical message they convey. Many who articulate what black people should do contend that America has been all bad for black people. They insist that the American tradition is unmitigated iniquity, that there have been no humanizing moments for either black or white people, and that there has been no progress in uplifting the downtrodden. Some even contend that the black man today is as oppressed as he ever was—even under slavery. Such is not a totally true assessment.

However, it must be conceded that those black militants who contend that things are not as they ought to be are not totally without facts. And it should be noted that they are right in the following instances.

First of all, they are right in the sense that in all areas to which one might point to slight improvements, the changes have been tortuously too slow, too gradual, and discouragingly too incomplete. This is especially true of black-white relations in general and the achievement of minority group civil rights in particular.

Secondly, it must also not be without note that there are still

181

unprecedented evils that can be attributed to America's seeming success, but which are actually against the collective well-being of society itself. This point is made by those who contend that it may well be that America has come to the point that is beyond change in its technological pollution, in its tendency toward ecological disasters, as a result of industrial greed, and in its insensitivity to environmental purity. They may well be right. It is beyond the scope of this book to make such a conclusion.

Thirdly, there are others who contend that America's current will to war is so deep that the future may not be assured for those who otherwise could or ought be able to feel secure. Many economically secure black and white people are even now suggesting that American society has reached a point where there is a serious question as to whether enough meaningful reform is yet possible. Great numbers of successful black and white people are at one in their contention that no mere list of improvements can assuage the impact of the above deep-rooted evils.

Finally, many of the militant radicals and the more reasoned blacks, many of the most affluent white cultural dropouts, as well as the many other brands of revolutionaries are at one in their deep doubts as to whether America's political legal-economic machinery has the inner strength remaining to achieve the sufficient changes so urgently needed to turn the tide of evil.

While one may well not yet be ready to concede the fact that the American political, social, or economic systems are not too impossible to be changed, he must face the fact that it is not a simple act and that there must be a sufficient number of knowledgeable people who are ready to demand and work for the types of changes needed. Admittedly, the system itself must be changed and reformed within the framework of the present structures.

Black people may well ask what the future of minorities is in a political system committed to majority rule. What are the alternatives to oppressive majority rule? They are at one in their conclusions that if one's utopian hopes are not fully realized or realizable within the American system, he must be sufficiently assured that there are limits to the tyranny of the majority. This battle is being currently fought through the courts and the electoral system. More radical changes and reforms must be realized in the future if hope is to remain possible.

However, before black people decide for revolution under any banner, it may be well for them to recognize that there is a vast current freedom void within the present American system which has not yet been filled.

Such a conclusion brings us to the point of a fuller assessment of what has been called the freedom vacuum; it is that void to which some major attention should now be given.

## The Current Freedom Vacuums

All the activities that have gone on before, which we have labeled the black man's civil rights struggle, have had a profound effect upon America. All the changes are much too extensive and complex to enumerate here. It is enough to be reminded that the black man's civil rights struggle has not been without its fruits, both negative and positive. However, we are concerned within this context with only the positive aspects of the civil rights struggle for the simple reason that too many of the hard-won freedoms which can be attributed to the black man's struggle are not yet being fully utilized by many black people.

There are too many freedoms that are yet unclaimed by black people; they are the freedoms that were won at the expense of the physical well-being and life of many of the prior civil rights workers. Many of the older civil rights workers are either dead or were rendered ineffective by a mental fatigue that was acquired during the hard days of the struggle. These unclaimed freedoms have remained obscured or unnoticed because the current more militant black power phase of the civil rights movement has been for the most part negative; and such negations have caused many black people to become misled by the confused beliefs that black people could achieve liberation and freedom in isolation and quite apart from other citizens of the same culture.

The mere mention of a freedom vacuum is not to contend that the black man is yet considered an equal and that there are not still larger freedoms yet to be won; it is rather to contend that one has to acquire equality together rather than in an alien context of separate and apart. Many black people will disagree with such a conclusion, but, nevertheless, these conclusions do not contend that change must be won at the cost of identity. It is rather to say that black people must live in a cultural context.

Almost as though it had come without the black man's knowledge, a vast part of the world has now finally come to the point of partially accepting that he ought to be free, and yet he has not fully taken advantage of such a change in white thinking. It may well be that black people have not yet become aware of such a mind-set because they do not dare believe that such a change, even to a degree, is at all possible or true. To be free is an awesome responsibility; for to whom much is given, much more is required.

## An Assumed Posture of Freedom

Here one speaks not of words, but of positive, resolute, and confident actions which bespeak a new type of assumption. It is an assumed posture of freedom. Such a posture is needed because there is within such an assumption a power much greater than even physical force or violence; it is a radical action which assumes a belonging that violence does not assume. Violence seeks to *achieve* a place for people rather than assume one. An assumed posture of freedom is a qualitative type of assumption or action, perhaps not heretofore a part of the civil rights strategy. It is to assume a new posture and to make a bold radical new assumption which causes one to act as a free agent on an assumption that is in excess of reality. To put it in another light, what would it mean for white America if black people were to assume a new role by the mere assumption of a freedom status which they thought heretofore had to be won by means of struggle, bitterness, violence, and conflict. It is the contention of this book that there are many unclaimed freedoms which have belonged to black people traditionally and which have already been won; they are, rather, the given and also the leftover freedoms from the civil rights struggle. They are broad freedoms which have not yet been claimed for two reasons. First, they are not now and have not ever been quite as visible as they might have, had they been sought openly and achieved by direct actions. Secondly, and more importantly so, it is because they are and always were there as the result of the inability of denying the fact that they were always there as rights of black as well as white people. To be more specific, currently there are hundreds of jobs that can be acquired by black people just for the asking; these are jobs which have not been heretofore open to black people. They are now given to white people only because there are not enough blacks who are willing and bold enought to assert their rights within the new job markets. We see black people on new jobs every day as an expression of this new climate. In political life, there are too few blacks who offer themselves for public office by pressing the total cause of the community. Many who have done so have been surprised that they have been elected by black and white support at both the national and local levels.

Almost any major university in the country will accept black students, but too few black students now apply. One gets the impression that too many blacks who now apply do not fully realize the full extent of their opportunity or their obligations to the black community and to the total national climate. It is sad that too much time is now being wasted on too many small and unimportant things on both black and white campuses. Many black students on white campuses are too busy attempting to acquire separate quarters, special considerations, and special attention to the neglect of real scholarship and the acquisition of adequate educational skills. There is a serious question as to whether much that is currently called for as special educational needs for black people can be considered a contribution to their ultimate liberation and freedom rather than a mere means to further their deeper enslavement. It cannot be contested that educational opportunities, even on the black college and university campuses, are not now being fully utilized. The black liberation struggle cannot ignore the need for adequate educational skills.

Big business is such that it is impossible for small black businesses to compete in many areas. If economic reforms are to be made, many of them must come from within the structures of big business itself. One welcomes new, bigger, and better black businesses. However, one must not overlook the fact that there are many broader opportunities now available within the structure of big business than blacks are ready to concede. Big business still is where the money is, and money is still a part of the success cycle of our culture. The above are just a few examples of the freedoms which are already won, but it is sad that they remain too often among the unclaimed.

Any assumed freedom must come to grips with the many opportunities which have already been won, and surely it must include a consideration of all the opportunities which are now open and are now made available to black people—to say nothing of the opportunities yet to be won.

Indeed, such assumptions of freedom would mean different and more radical actions, and such freedom assumptions would call for a change of the black man's attitude toward his current place and status in America. It would and could mean no less than an assumption that he belongs here and that he plans to confront any and all conditions which would challenge his right to stay and derive the full benefits from total America. It is the contention of this book that such an assumed posture of freedom, at this point in history, would be hard to frustrate.

## Positive Value in Such an Assumed Posture of Freedom

It must be pointed out and conceded that any assumption of freedom, any radical new actions on the part of black people, would require a new kind of thinking that is totally alien to the modern man of conquest. It is past the time for such bold assertion for the simple reason that conditions are now right. Black people have talked too long of oppressions that simply do not now exist; they still talk of oppressions far in excess of the current reality. Now it would seem that many black people are using such assertions as a mere means of escape. This is especially true considering the fact that oppression is still a very grave and present reality. But it is also possible to overstate the facts as they are.

Have not all oppressed people of every period tried too often to forget

> that man is truly existent, real, contemporary with himself, acquiescent and certain? Memory binds him to the past that no longer is. Hope casts him upon the future that is not yet. He remembers having lived, but he does not live. He remembers having loved, but he does not love. He remembers having the thoughts of others, but he does not think. It seems to be the same with him in hope. He hopes to live, but he does not live. He expects to be happy one day, and this expectation causes him to pass over the happiness of the present. He is never, in memory and hope, wholly himself and wholly in his present. Always he either limps behind it or hastens ahead of it. Memories and hope appear to cheat him of the happiness of being undividedly present. They rob him of his present and drag him into times that no longer exist or do not yet exist. They surrender him to the nonexistent and abandon him to vanity. For these times subject him to the stream of transcience—the stream that sweeps him to annihilation.[1]

[1] Moltmann, *The Theology of Hope* (New York: Harper & Row, 1967), p. 26.

What is needed within the black community, and surely within the larger American context, is for black people to assume a bond and radical new posture of freedom which would transform their pilgrimage toward equal status from a negative to a positive approach. It would be a posture much more mature than merely the asking for freedom. It would be one of assuming that one is free; and surely it would also include one of claiming that facet of one's freedom that is now unclaimed.

To so act means that one assumes a prior attitude of freedom; when one assumes a prior attitude of freedom, one makes a positive, mature effort to live as a free person. One does not have to be rude or uncivilized to claim what is his by right. One needs not be unkind to be realistic about or critical of anyone or of anything that frustrates such a posture. One should and must be against anyone who attempts to act as if such is not the case. To so act means that one is willing and ready to compete with any other peer, black or white, in an open and fully competitive arena. To so act means that one assumes an equal mind-set that will not accept anything other than a status which is equal.

The freedom stance referred to above does not presuppose that there will be no need for future actions such as protests, conflicts, confrontations, or even possible revolution. It is no more than a persistent and positive calling for a consolidation of many of the gains that have already been won, but which have yet to be claimed by black people. The horizon of expectations within the black community needs to be lifted above the current state of mere negative complaints. Conduct from such a frame of reference must be developed and predicated upon the utopian ideal that one is already free and that freedom is an unalienable right, first for self and then for all others. One must always leave a place within his thinking that both self and the other must have the room in which to be free. If the current black person is to assume a posture of freedom, he can never adjust to or allow the preservation of the existing social and judicial orders if these do not allow for the freedom of one's self and others. In this sense, then, to assume a posture that will lay claim on the reality of the moment in a given time and a given place is a position that needs not be achieved or bought by adjusting to what is the case; it is to assume a position of what should be.

An adequate assumed posture of freedom must have at least three positive values for black people. First of all, there must be inherent within it a deep principle and basic truth. It must be a truth that has already internalized the freedom upon which such a posture must rest. Such a posture must express the essence of both black and white people. It must express the inner aim of the mutual existence of all personhood; it must be representative of what man essentially is. It must express a sense of inner freedom that is a manifestation of what man has as an inner aim and what he must have for his future fulfillment as a person. Such an assumed posture of freedom is valid for a black person's individual existence just as much as it is valid for his social existence, and it may well be impossible to claim or understand one without the other. An assumed posture of freedom loses its truth unless it motivates one to self-fulfillment and directs his actions toward the ultimate fulfillment of the larger social order.

Secondly, such an assumed posture of freedom must assume a fruitfulness which stands in close relationship to its truth. Such a positive freedom assumption opens up the fruitful possibilities that would have otherwise remained hidden if not seen by such positive anticipations. Where such a mature position is not present, where no anticipating assumptions open up possibilities, there is only to be found a decadent present, not only in individuals, but also in a whole nation of people. Where there is no such anticipating assumptions, the self-realization of individual human possibilities also tend to remain stifled.

A third positive characteristic of such an assumed posture of freedom should make it impossible to imprison the person who has assumed such a posture. A person so obsessed will not accept prison. Here such an individual or collective assumption is to be equated with the great utopian movements which have revolutionalized the world. As an example, Judaism is perhaps the most momentous utopian movement of human history, for directly and indirectly it has elevated all mankind to another sphere of existence on the basis of its utopian ideal of the coming reign of God. Such a freedom posture must for the black man result in a hope that is unwilling to accept any external conditions that would make such an assumption extinguishable. There is no political or social reality that should be able to change such a state of inner commitment to an attitude of an assumed freedom for the simple reason that such an assumption is already the future taking place in the present. Such an assumption is the sample of the not yet of a fuller future reality that has not yet arrived. Such an assumption is also an assumed posture of freedom claimed by a person who will not allow who he is, and what he may become, to be determined by the present evil world; rather, his being will be determined by the vision that has grown out of common personal and collective longings and higher personal and collective aspirations. Thus, for a people to assume such a freedom is a sign that they have already internalized the possibilities of a social order based on the sheer strength of the new assumptions mentioned above. It posture presupposes that freedom is the will to creativity that the total community embodies within itself. It presupposes a communal discipline for the sake of the future. And this calls for a people or a person already liberated, a liberated person who is large enough to occupy freedom's larger space.

Finally, such an assumed freedom stance calls for a black person, a black people, of a new spirit, of a new breed; it calls for a black people who have settled some of the primary concerns which now trouble the current black community. It calls for a black person with a new kind of maturity that has not been determined by the current maze of political, social, and moral crises. Such a freedom assumption calls for a black people who will accept the challenge of the volatile nature of our current circumstances and transform them into a new day for black people on the sheer strength of the new assumptions mentioned above. It is an assumption of a new and higher maturity. In his *Paradise Lost,* Milton reminds us that "the mind is its own place, and in itself can make a Heaven or Hell, and a Hell or Heaven." It is such a concept of the mind that is assumed here. Such an assumption calls for one to live by the love of what he may never see. Such is the secret of the needed inner discipline. Such a call for a new type of black person is a call for a new inner spirit which will refuse to let the creative act of a new assumption be dissolved away in immediate sense experiences. Such disciplined assumptions of freedom are what have traditionally given prophets, revolutionaries, and saints the courage to die for the future they envisaged.

## The Ultimate Option of Hope

The ultimate option for the black Christian, as for any other Christian, is the option of hope. Not to hope is not to live by faith in current modern and difficult times. There is no other option for the black Christian because of the nature of his faith. His faith is and must be in a better tomorrow, a tomorrow which presupposes a kind of utopian future not totally achieved by mere human striving. And yet, while much within America has been achieved in the way of creature comforts, so much more is yet to be desired. More than that, and in spite of the present, there is so much that is dreamed of, even demanded, which is not yet a reality—such as a future beyond human conflict where all attitudes are positive and committed to what is right for self and right for others. However, when one bears the added burden of a self that is physically different, he cannot help but conclude that to be black is an added burden. So for the black man, who is physically different, there may well be the added need for the development of an ethic of hope with an added dimension. If one concedes that hope is one of the basic spiritual ingredients that serves to enhance the quality of human life wherever it is found, then it follows that life without a hope is but a caricature of the divine gift of a creation about which Christian literature so dramatically and cogently speaks. Surely void of hope, no black person can assume a posture of freedom; he would be void of the needed inner strength.

Religion's hope has always been characterized by a desire to become part of what is ongoing. At the same time, one cannot concede that every new development ultimately becomes a part of the future or is later adopted as being characteristic of the future that has become the now of time. The effects of hope are ultimately judged by the changes they have helped to achieve in the life of a people. The goal of black Christian hope is symbolic of a permanent revival, not a mere temporary alteration which washes off when the excitement is gone. Traditionally, amid all that was not right, amid all that was against them and the future, black people have dared to hope. Hope amid utter despair has been the central quality of the black religious experience. Probably no better words can be found for this context than words penned by an alien, atheistic philosopher, Ernst Bloch, who contends:

> We live and do not know why. We die and do not know whither. To say what one wants now and afterwards is easy. But no one can say what he wants at all in this so very purposive existence. "I wonder why I am of good cheer," says an adage carved into medieval doors.
>
> And yet we here, suffering and benighted, can hope far afield. If it remains strong enough, if it is pure and undistractedly aware of itself, hope will not fail us. For the human soul encompasses all things, even the beyond that is not yet. The soul alone is what we want, and thinking serves it. It is the sole space of thought, the content of its language, and its object—an object . . . concealed in the darkness of the lived moment.[2]

[2] Ernst Bloch, *Man on His Own* (New York: Herder and Herder, 1970), p. 69.

Bloch can furnish only the worded expression for black people, for traditionally black people in America have had a faith of their own, and their hope has been from a Christian faith frame of reference rather than from a mere rational atheistic frame of reference. God has traditionally been more for black people than against them. For this reason, black people have had reason to hope and to celebrate.

This book is offered to remind us all, black and white, that the future may well belong to those who hope for the simple reason that they are the only people who have something to live for. We have come to a time when black people live among white people who seemingly, from the way they now act, are so fearful of black people that they may become more repressive and fearful rather than understanding what is taking place within the black community. White people have lived so long as the oppressors, with a mythological fear of black people, that the fear has now seemingly become an obsession with all too many. Too many white people have become the slaves of a traditional master complex without realizing it. Their prison is without walls or keepers, for the black man has never been nor ever wanted to be the keeper of the white man's prison. He traditionally has been too trustful of his white oppressors. This is yet too much a part of his mind-set.

The white person of our time needs to keep company with the real black man who is fully equipped to keep company with him as an equal. Too many white people have not known the black man of hope. They have not met the new black man of an assumed posture of freedom; they do not yet know the reality of a liberated black man. One would suspect that white people dread the day when the real black man will stand up. It would seem that just for the asking there is a new role awaiting the new black man of hope—if he would but assume it. It is a role which would free himself *and* the ex-master. It is the role of being an equal to the person who does not recognize the fact that history has already

193

mandated such a posture. It is to this new role that the last pages of this book would call both white and black people of tomorrow.

## The Positive Aspects of an Ethic of Hope

The black man of hope who assumes the new freedom posture rooted in an ethic of hope cannot remain preoccupied with hate or with exaggerated overstatements of conditions as they now exist for black people. This is not the same as saying he should be unrealistic. To the contrary, equally important will be the need for an ever objective, an ever realistic understanding of the current issues of his time. The new black man of hope will not be an unrealistic dreamer. He will have to be a man who stands taller than the current hour. The dynamics of his life of faith and his fix on a new kind of hope will need to be such that it will always be impossible to determine with any degree of precision where his hope ends and where his faith really begins.

Indeed, the Christian ethic has always been essentially an ethic of hope; its context of realization is the now and the not yet; the oppressive struggle coexists with the consciousness of victory as realized in an ultimate eschatological future not-yet event. That is why the delay in the manifestations of the fruits of hope do not now or ever detract from the intensity of a genuinely Christian ethical endeavor. The boundary between faith and hope melts away since faith affirms the reality of the present and hope affirms the future reality of that which is hoped for as though it were something already present. But neither is faith affirmed nor hope invoked or sustained without the last full measure of human effort expended in the never-ending attempt to eradicate anything that would frustrate human fulfillment and self-realization.

Faith in God cannot be fully realized without giving some thought to God's creation as one condition for accepting God and affirming a positive faith and hope. One has to relate to God's creation as a part of the given because this is where he must live

194

out his earthly existence. One important facet of God's creation is one's neighbor. It is within reason to conclude that since man is such an important part of God's creation, one cannot hope unless he accepts the fact that he must come to terms with neighbor. One accepts his neighbor in the degree to which he accepts directing his efforts to the neighbor's welfare. Man in faith is man for others. Assumed liberation and assumed freedom cannot manifest themselves in glory and power over others, but rather must find themselves in self-giving and love for others. It must be noted that faith is at stake here in that it is impossible to love another person unless at the same time one can regard that person as one for whom one must accept or assume some responsibility. When we trust God in faith, when we affirm neighbor as a part of our responsibility, we experience a freedom and serenity in our being that is akin to the experience we feel in the consciousness of our self-identification with the object of our love in self-surrender and service. To affirm neighbor, to serve the neighbor means to identify yourself with him, in doing for him that which he cannot do for himself. This is why the black man must; it is why he cannot find the way to liberation and a larger freedom for himself without also finding the way to liberation and freedom for his white brother. To be fully liberated and free means for both a break with a past master-slave tradition that has long since enslaved them both.

## The Transformation Power of a Utopian Hope

All who have come to this point in their reading and assessment of this work will have fully recognized that it has been written from a stubborn frame of reference that is consistently oriented toward an optimism that looks to an eschatological future under God. One must already have sensed that this book presupposes that such an ethic for black theology and the currently unfolding politics of liberation must be deeply rooted in the now and the not yet. Eschatology, so conceived, must be understood as the teaching about the relation of all things to the last thing or, as it were, about the lastness of all things.[3]

A Christian eschatology, relevant to black theology and to the politics of liberation, can be neither a tentative guess at how fragmented gains may be achieved nor a specific program of immediate utopia; it is rather the lighting up of a new dimension of life now. It is meant to introduce into the present a new astringency and a new urgency. As has been said again and again, if the black man's search for a usable future is to be fruitful, it must be seasoned with an eschatological hope that is utopian enough to lift him above the current state of frustration, despair, confusion, lack of direction, a growing bitterness, and a deep hate that is too widespread within the black community. Indeed, it may well be that black history could best serve black people if those who now teach it would attempt to develop a new stance toward a "new past." It may be that the old past for too many current black people is frozen by a kind of false conception of black history that has resulted in a kind of totally negative regret or contempt for the black experience and all that it has meant for black people within American culture. To so view the black experience is never to be able in the future to say to white America as did Joseph, the ancient Jew of old, to his brothers in Egypt: You meant it all for evil, but God helped me transform it all to my own glory and good. Not to view the black experience in some such positive sense is to fail by missing its important deeper religious meaning. What is it if it is not the prior African religious and cultural background of the slave fused with what he accepted of a Christianity that had been diluted, distorted, and conditioned by a pro-white American culture. The black religious experience is the purer elements of each fused into a new and fresh religious appropriation.

[3] Evgenil Lampert, *The Apocalypse of History* (London: Faber & Faber, 1948), p. 14.

One must recall, first of all, that utopian hope has always been a transforming element in the black religious experience. It has always rejected an insipid faith and an insensitive ethic by holding faith and ethics together in a life of courage in suffering and hope, of suffering in courage and hope, and hope in courage and suffering. Existentially, all men of utopian hope have transformed history; they have not been transformed by history. Theologically, whenever one views the now in relation to the not yet of the future, his view takes on new dimensions. He sees everything from an eschatological perspective. It is as though one is looking at history from the end. The fashion of this world looks different when seen from the end. The neutrality goes out of it. It is as though the beam of a searchlight has been turned upon it, immeasureably deepening the contrast between the light and the dark. The flatness is taken from living. A new edge and tone is given to it. The common round becomes charged with fresh moment and decisiveness.

This was the spirit of the early days of the civil rights movement; it was something of the theological and ethical breath that Dr. Martin Luther King, Jr., breathed into it. The Birmingham jail was surely equal to Attica, but because his hope was utopian, the Birmingham jail became the occasion for one of the greatest letters of modern times. For the blacks at Attica, it was an occasion of death and ultimate annihilation. Blacks at Attica had lost hope. Utopian hope is transforming for the simple reason that it makes it possible for the person of hope to reject injustice without ceasing to acclaim the nature of man and the beauty of this world. It is precisely this necessary hope that too many people in the black community so desperately lack. The more frightening thing is that so many people of the modern world, black and white, have begun to seek outlets in mere man-made eschatologies, only to find that such decisions are but attempts to recreate a lost sense of each moment as a day of decision. It is a vain attempt to restore the pinch of expectancy to lives which

197

have long ago lost the will to hope and have become dead and insipid.

Utopian hope is transforming, secondly, because it never becomes blind to the reality of the now of history; its burning desire for a better future never prevents the person of hope from savoring the reality of the now; it rather allows the person of the now to taste the fresh fruits of what he hopes for in the future. Could it be that Martin Luther King, Jr., really did taste and see the reality of the future on the occasion of his last speech before his death? Indeed, his actions and his words would give such an impression. Utopian hope is transforming because it allows one to live in the now of today and, occasionally, also to live in the tomorrow which has not yet come.

Utopian hope is transforming because its eschatological dimensions represent a future-oriented, expectant stance; its reality is always out of step with the assumptions of the era; otherwise, it becomes banal. The God of utopian hope comes to man always as the disturber of his peace. He comes as the one who will not allow him to settle down to what is. One so aware senses that the future is always under God, and that such a future under God always, without exceptions, commits one to what should be.

Christian eschatological hope can be meaningful in the black community only if it is recognized for what it is. Utopian hope as an eschatological Christian hope is not fulfilled automatically, but only as black people give themselves up in active commitment and hope and planning for its realization. The center of such a hope is this: that black people will never find or think themselves in an absolutely impossible situation. There will and there should always be a hope that there is a possibility of an opening to a new future under God. There must always be the faith that the God of the future will transmute folly and even death into atonement and ultimate resurrection. Hope, thus conceived, makes it a powerful energizing force for Christian moral, social, and political aspirations. To be sure, the man of hope must in times of disorder live at the level of reality; however, his hope stance should without exception point to another order, a newer day to come, which should always prevent him from being completely content with the present.

Finally, utopian hope is transforming because it is a formless hope, void of a full and final content. It is a hope which always exceeds one's grasp. It is always in search of a fuller content. It is a hope that some fuller form of hope will one day be made available to persons who would otherwise despair. Too many black people, especially those who tend to despair, take current reality as final. It may well be that there are too few people of hope and planning who are interested in doctoring up the current system, but who are rather at work preparing for a superior reality that will replace that which is current. A new day will come when, under God, such a hope summons a new black people to stand up! Such a summons is not of God if it does not bid one to stand as an equal in the collective company of all of God's children.

# Bibliography

Arendt, Hannah. *On Revolution*. New York: Viking Press, 1965.

Baldwin, James. *The Fire Next Time*. New York: Delta Books, 1964.

Barclay, William. *Ethics in a Permissive Society*. New York: Harper & Row, 1971.

Bergor, Peter, and Neubus, Richard. *Movement and Revolution: On American Radicalism*. Garden City, N.Y.: Doubleday & Co., 1970.

Bloch, Ernst. *Man on His Own*. Translated by James W. Leitch. New York: Harper & Row, 1967.

Braaten, Carl E. *Christ and Counter-Christ*. Philadelphia: Fortress Press, 1972.

Brandon, S. G. F. *Jesus and the Zealots*. New York: Stein & Day, 1968.

Camus, Albert. *The Rebel: An Essay on Man in Revolt*. Translated by Anthony Bower. New York: Random House, 1956.

Cleage, Albert B. *The Black Messiah*. New York: Sheed & Ward, 1968.

Cone, James H. *A Black Theology of Liberation*. Philadelpia: J. B. Lippincott Co., 1970.

———. *Black Theology and Black Power*. New York: The Seabury Press, 1969.

Cox, Harvey. *The Feast of Fools*. Cambridge, Mass.: Harvard University Press, 1969.

———. *The Secular City*. New York: The Macmillan Co., 1965.

Cullmann, Oscar. *Jesus and the Revolutionaries*. New York: Harper & Row, 1970.

DeWolf, L. Harold. *Responsible Freedom: Guidelines for Christian Action*. New York: Harper & Row, 1971.

———. "Public and Private Dimensions of Ethical Responsibility." In *Toward a Discipline of Social Ethics: Essays in Honor of Walter G. Muelder,* edited by Paul Deats, Jr. Boston, Mass.: Boston University Press, 1972.

DuBois, W. E. B. *Black Reconstruction in America*. New York: World Publishing Co., 1964.

Edwards, George R. *Jesus and the Politics of Violence*. New York: Harper & Row, 1972.

Ellul, Jacques. *Violence*. New York: The Seabury Press, 1969.

Fair, Ronald. "Symposium on Black Power." *Negro Digest,* November, 1966, p. 94.

Fanon, Frantz, *The Wretched of the Earth*. New York: Grove Press, 1966.

———. *Black Skins, White Masks*. Translated by C. L. Markmann. New York: Grove Press, 1967.

Fitch, Robert E. "The Use of Violence." *The Christian Century,* April, 1968.

Gaustad, Edwin Scott. *A Religious History of America*. New York: Harper & Row, 1966.

Genet, Jean. Article in *Ramparts,* June, 1970, p. 31.

Goldston, Robert. *The Negro Revolution*. New York: The Macmillan Co., 1968.

Gustafson, James M. *Christ and the Moral Life*. New York: Harper & Row, 1968.

Harding, Vincent. "The Religion of Black Power." In *The Religious Situation: 1968*, edited by Donald R. Cutler. Boston: Beacon Press, 1968.

Hazelton, Roger. *The God We Worship*. New York: The Macmillan Co., 1946.

Jones, Major J. *Black Awareness: A Theology of Hope*. Nashville: Abingdon Press, 1971.

Killens, John Oliver. "Symposium on Black Power." *Negro Digest*, November, 1966.

King, Martin Luther, Jr., *Where Do We Go from Here: Chaos or Community?* New York: Harper & Row, 1967.

―――. *Strength to Love*. New York: Harper & Row, 1959.

―――. "Pilgrimage to Non-Violence." *Christian Century*, April 13, 1960.

Lampert, E. *The Apocalypse of History*. London: Faber & Faber, 1948.

Lehmann, Paul. *Ethics in a Christian Context*. New York: Harper & Row, 1963.

Lincoln, C. Eric. *Sounds of Struggle: Persons and Perspectives in Civil Rights*. New York: Friendship Press, 1967.

Lorenz, Konrad. *On Aggression*. New York: Harcourt, Brace and World, 1966.

Lovell, John. *Black Song: The Forge and the Flame*. New York: The Macmillan Co., 1972.

Macquarrie, John. *Principles of Christian Theology*. New York: Charles Scribner's Sons, 1966.

Mays, Benjamin. *The Negro's God*. New York: Atheneum, 1968.

Meadows, Chris M. "A Constructive View of Anger, Aggression, and Violence." *Pastoral Psychology*, September, 1971, pp. 9 ff.

Moberly, Walton. *Responsibility*. Greenwich, Conn.: The Seabury Press, 1956.

Moltmann, Jürgen. *Religion, Revolution and the Future*. Translated by M. Douglas Meeks. New York: Charles Scribner's Sons, 1969.

————. *Hope and Planning*. Translated by Margaret Clarkson. New York: Harper & Row, 1971.

————. *Theology of Hope*. Translated by James W. Leitch. New York: Harper & Row, 1967.

Montague, M. F. Ashley, ed. *Man and Aggression*. New York: Oxford University Press, 1968.

Morris, Colin. *Unyoung, Uncolored, Unpoor*. New York: Abingdon Press, 1969.

Muse, Benjamin. *The American Negro Revolution: From Non-Violence to Black Power*. New York: Citadel Press, 1968.


Ramsey, Paul. *Deeds and Rules in Christian Ethics*. New York: Charles Scribner's Sons, 1967.

————. *Christian Ethics and the Sit-In*. New York: Association Press, 1961.

————. "The Morality of Abortion." in *Life or Death: Ethics and Options,* edited by Daniel H. Libby. P. 71.

Riccoeur, Paul. *History and Truth*. Evanston Ill.: Northwestern University Press, 1965.

Roberts, David E. *Psychotherapy and a Christian View of Man.* New York: Charles Scribner's Sons, 1950.

Roberts, J. Deotis. *Liberation and Reconciliation: A Black Theology*. Philadelphia: The Westminister Press, 1971.


Scott, John Paul. "The Anatomy of Violence." In *Violence in the Streets,* edited by Shalom Endleman. Chicago: Quadrangle Books, 1968.

Shaull, Richard, and Oglesby, Carl. *Containment and Change*. New York: The Macmillan Co., 1967.

Shils, Edward. "The Sanctity of Life." In *Life or Death: Ethics and Options,* edited by Daniel H. Libby. Seattle, Wash.: University of Washington Press, 1968.


Thomas, George F. *Christian Ethics and Moral Philosophy*. New York: Charles Scribner's Sons, 1955.

Tillich, Paul. *The Courage to Be*. New Haven: Yale University Press, 1952.

Willams, Daniel Day. *The Spirit and the Forms of Love*. New York: Harper & Row, 1968.

Wogaman, J. Philip. "The Dilemma of Christian Social Strategy." In *Toward a Discipline of Social Ethics*, edited by Paul Deats, Jr. Boston: Boston University Press, 1972.